conversational style, the book is eminently readable, frequently bringing a smile with one of his pithy one-liners or his illustrative anecdotes. This book adds to his credentials of being a youth leader. He may be a retired coach, but he hasn't stopped coaching. He has another winner in this book.

Joseph Wood, instructor,
Lansing Community College

A natural way with words, wisdom, a sense of humor, and a colorful mind is a great mixture in creating these unique readings that offer insightful, useful, witty, and wise information to help make each of us a better person. People today are so busy there isn't enough time to read. Tom's book offers fun reading for whatever time people have to spare. Reading his book for just a few moments gives a chuckle, yet also provides a great life lesson!

Sandra Thoney, author
Iron River, Michigan

Coach Tom Swanson hits another home run with his latest book! Reading this book is like sitting at the knee of your grandfather as he lovingly gives you advice and imparts stories and yarns; wonderful words to live by. I encourage you to take a seat, get comfortable, and drink in Tom's sage wisdom, chin in the palms of your hands, as I did. Thanks, Coach!

Kathy Dobie
Former student, Potterville High School,
Potterville, Michigan

You don't have to be old in order to be wise! In his book, Tom gives a simple, easy-to-read rundown on how to be not only smart, but also a wise person. It's like having your own personal "pocket mentor" who's "been there done that," helping you navigate through life and make the most of it.

Katya Baxter, Young Life kid
Businesswoman, new mom

I really like reading Tom's thoughts in his new book. It has short pieces that I can take with me for the day that are tied directly to the scriptures. I believe Tom has done it again and you will completely enjoy this book.

Don Nesbitt, Central Region Director
Meridian Joint School District No. 2

What a unique book of encouragement! There is gold on every page. To get started in a new and positive direction, this book is an absolute must. You will love the "Coffee Breaks."

Tom Shoquist
President, The Eureka Foundation
Trustee, LeTourneau Unversity

Tom and Donna Swanson
(photo by Chad Case Photography)

BLOWING your KNOWS in PUBLIC:

From Smart to Wise

Tom Swanson
aka "Professor OB1 Kaswanni"

SF
Simple Faith Books
Boise, ID

BLOWING YOUR KNOWS IN PUBLIC
Published by Simple Faith Books
A division of Sunrise Mountain Books
www.sunrisemountainbooks.com
13347 W. Tapatio Drive
Boise, ID 83713

Because most of the one-liners in this book came from so many
unconventional sources over a period of many years, proper footnotes
are impossible. Many one-liners have been used so frequently they
have become part of the oral tradition and now are archived in the
wisdom of the common man. Attempts were made to identify the origin
of these sayings wherever possible. The author is grateful for the
original authors and speakers who shared their wisdom and insights
now recorded in this work, and will gladly give credit in subsequent
editions should the original sources be identified.

Cartoon light bulb image by Cory Thoman, licensed from ClipArtOf.com.
Cartoon coffee guy image by Ron Leishman licensed from ClipArtOf.com

ISBN 978-0-9842362-3-7
First printing 2013

Printed in the UNITED STATES OF AMERICA

With love, hugs, and eternal thanks

To those very special folks who demonstrated to me that
wisdom can be lived out every day:

My parents
Lester and Viola Swanson

And my in-laws
John and Nell Serena

The next generations will attempt to follow
your most excellent example.

*"Today you are you,
that is truer than true;
there is no one alive
who is Youer than you!"*

Dr. Seuss

*"Learn to be wise and develop good
judgment and common sense! I cannot
overemphasize this point. Cling to
Wisdom—she will protect you. Love her—
she will guard you!"* Proverbs 4:5-6 TLB

CONTENTS

Foreword
Preface
Acknowledgments
Certificate
From Smart ... 20
To Wise ... 21
*Coffee Break ... 22
Introduction ... 23
*Coffee Break ... 31

SECTION 1 **Will you Quit Listening to the "Know- It-Alls?" ... 32**
  Should ... 38
  What If? ... 39
  Not Fair! ... 40
  Why Me? ... 41
  I Was Gunna, But... 42
  Good Old Days ... 43
  *Coffee Break ... 44

SECTION 2 **Is it Time to Sign the Eviction Notice? ... 45**
  Forget ... 51
  Ought ... 52
  "Miserabling" ... 53
  "Awfulizing" ... 54
  Perfection ... 55
  Experts ... 56
  *Coffee Break ... 57

SECTION 3 **What Have You Learned in the "School of Hard Knocks?" ...58**

   Snookered ...62
   Life's Tough ...63
   Critics ...64
   Narcissists ...65
   Know-it-Alls ...66
   Process ...67
   *Coffee Break ...68

SECTION 4 **Will What Got You Here Get You Where You Want to Go? ...69**

   Look Back ...75
   Look Forward ...76
   Look Inside ...77
   Look Around ...78
   Look Out! ...79
   Look Above ...80
   *Coffee Break ...81

SECTION 5 **Does Waiting Work? ...82**

   Waiting ...86
   Waffling ...87
   Wandering ...88
   Will Power! ...89
   For What? ...90
   Move it! ...91
   *Coffee Break ...92

SECTION 6 **Can Bad News Be Good News? ...93**

   Reality ...97
   Gut Check ...98

Perspective ...99
Possible ...100
Probable ...101
Predictable ...102
Profitable ...103
*Coffee Break ...104

SECTION 7 **Can You Encourage Your Confidence? ...105**
Optimism ...110
Hope ...111
Effervescence ...112
Stability ...113
Persistence ...114
Smarts ...115
*Coffee Break ...116

SECTION 8 **Are You a Smart Aleck or a Wise guy? ...118**
Discriminate ...122
Believe ...123
Sincerity ...124
Anchors ...125
Political Correctness ...126
Wisdom ...124
*Coffee Break ...127

SECTION 9 **Is the Most Important Thing You Do Next? ... 129**
Prioritize ...133
Action ...134
Timing ...135
Strategy ...136
Paradigm ...137

Self-Talk ...138
*Coffee Break ...139

SECTION 10 **Let's Get Moving from Smart
to Wise ...140**
Who ...144
What ...145
When ...146
Where ...147
How ...148
Why ...149
*Coffee Break ...150

SECTION 11 **Will You Listen to Him?
Who's "Him?"..151**
Reality ...166
Know Your Place ...167
Curious ...168
Download ...169
Digest ...170
Activate! ...171
Come! ...172
Follow! ...173
Me ...174
Rejoice! ...175
*Coffee Break ...176

FAREWELL **"Knows Up!"** ... 177

Why Books, Wood Crafts, and Quilts? ...181

Bibliography ...183

FOREWORD

We are constantly bombarded with excessive information and lists. We can find top ten's in best restaurants, best movies, best TV shows, and everything you can name. The problem is, we remember so little. But, we typically do remember humorous stories, one-liners, and catch phrases. What makes them stick?

Chip and Dan Heath have spent most of their academic lives researching what makes ideas stick. Why do similar proverbs circulate in every society generation after generation? What are the ideas that stick, and what makes them stick? Their book on why some ideas survive and others die is entitled *Made to Stick*. Keep it simple: minimum words. "It's the economy, stupid" (Bill Clinton). Emotion works: "If I hold one, I will act" (Mother Teresa). Stories as great influencers—Jared, the 425 pound fast food dieter for Subway (1998) on the theme "7 under 6," i.e., seven subs under six grams of fat. He lost nearly 250 pounds!!

Long before the Heath brothers wrote their books, Tom Swanson was saying, "If it clicks, it sticks." So whether it was ideas, legends, rumors, anecdotes, proverbs, mini-stories, word nuggets, or bumper sticker theology, all became part of Tom's life-long collection of one-liners. He learned that the proverb "where there's smoke there's fire" is found in at least fifty-five different languages. Different cultures, similar expressions, but universally understood truths.

Over twenty years ago, I was working on a book that remained untitled until it was completed. Tom took a look and suggested, "When Riding a Dead Horse, For Heaven's Sake, Dismount." Click. The title sold more books than did its content.

Without a doubt, you will find stories and one-liners in this book that are helpful, simple, emotional, and informative. Have fun, and remember, "Light yourself with the fire of enthusiasm and people will stand in line to watch you burn." Success is never the result of spontaneous combustion; you must set yourself on fire.

Dr. Barry Asmus,
Senior Economist,
National Center for Policy Analysis,
Author and speaker

"Professor OB1 Kaswanni" and His One-Liners

Blowing Your Knows In Public: From Smart to Wise comes in response to your very positive acceptance of my first book. Every first-time author accepts the uncertainty of how the reading public will respond. I just kept typing until GRADUATION: "So What Just Happened?" became a reality.

While typing, I kept reminding myself to do some of the things I was encouraging my readers. It was an adventure into uncharted territory. It really was playing my hunches, keeping on writing and rewriting, *"fuss, fiddle, and fixing,"* and re-reading to try and figure out what I had just written.

My attitude has always been somewhat "if they can do it, I can do it!" Leaving a trail of wrecked bikes, busted skis, and numerous aches and pains taught me lessons where my excessive ambition needed to be cautioned with some wisdom and experience. Having never run cross-country or wrestled, when asked to start and coach a team, I said yes, and figured it out on the fly, producing many successful athletes.

For several years as we parked in the church parking lot in Mason, Michigan, we never missed seeing a homemade snowmobile trailer parked next door. The plywood carpentry left much to be desired. The paint choice must have been intentionally ugly because it demonstrated the truth of the statement hand-painted across the side:

"In great attempts it is glorious even to fail!"

Be encouraged! Once I committed to taking my first steps of starting to write, it was most encouraging the number of friends who added their expertise to help start my blog. That led to suggestions, encouragement, and help in the publishing process.

The encouragement and enthusiastic response to my first book led to many conversations about doing another book, even going so far as to suggest one-liners and topics for this book. You can guess the source of the title idea? Thanks to the one who first commented:

A wise man never blows his knows in public.

Sometime after the 1976 cross-country season where Potterville, Michigan High School won the boys' and girls' Class D state championship, the mother of two sons and a daughter who ran for me gave me a hand-painted plaque:

If "ifs" and "buts" were candy and nuts, we'd all have a merry Christmas!

As a team, on our journey to the state championship, they had come to learn that

*our "ifs" would not produce results. They
also learned that our "buts" were just
excuses. They had committed to this little
one liner. NO ifs! NO buts! Everyone
competed to do their best and let the results
speak for themselves. I was so proud of their
wisdom and determination to succeed.*

The excitement and my surprise over the years are
the stories, Facebook posts, emails, personal notes, and
greetings that so often contain a one-liner from the past.
My use of one-liners was never intended as teaching. I
was just passing on an interesting comment. They must
have clicked, because they were remembered.

*As a junior high youngster, I happened to
glance at a little 3x5 sign on a bulletin
board. My life was instantly changed. That
idea planted the seed of the effectiveness of
a one liner:*

Life is a tough teacher:
first you get the test, then you get the
lesson!

Somehow, it just "clicked!" When something clicks
in your mind it "sticks!" You don't have to work at
learning it, you just did. In many ways it has become the
way I think, live, teach, and coach.

Blowing Your Knows in Public started with a one-
liner. It energized my thinking about how you can
transform your life by training your thinking to move
from Smart To Wise.

Through attending "The School of Hard Knocks," your "knows" have expanded greatly. Now the transition from "smart to wise" continues. Hopefully, you can master skill at living.

Saying so don't make it so!

Ideas "stick" when they "click!" Get ready for many "aha" moments when these one-liners, which might be new to you, instantly "click." The one-liners can become your new favorite professor. You are unique. Your "knows" belong individually to you. How you respond, react, and apply what you will be reading can become the *new you*, or could just become another book on your shelf.

Life can only be understood looking backwards;
it can only be lived going forwards.

While every one of us "graduate" to each new day, hopefully *Blowing Your Knows In Public* will challenge your thinking anew so that you really start focusing on transforming *From Smart To Wise*.

It's what you learn after you know it all that counts.

My motivation and anticipation is that Blowing Your Knows In Public will really encourage your thinking and empower you to move on *From Smart To Wise.*

Don't expect a lot of instant answers. Your thought process and self talk will be directed to rethink and reformulate your action steps going forward. I hope you become an exceptional student, wanting to direct yourself toward wisdom and excellence.

*You can lead a human to knowledge,
but you can't make them think.*

Be encouraged! Understand that *possibility* is always ahead. You *can* process your life, thinking and behaviors. You *can* evaluate your present thinking and responses to life. You *can* rethink and reconnect with better action steps leading to improvement. As Dr. Seuss said so brilliantly, *"There is no one alive who is Youer than you!"* Challenge yourself: *"I will be the best me I can be!"* Carry on!

You are never too old to chart a new course!

☆ ☆ ☆

Note: Recommendation for Mental Health Professionals

I am a retired teacher and coach who has been interested in helping students, family and friends mature into fully functioning adults. In some cases, trained mental health professionals are required to help that process continue successfully. "Professor OB1 Kaswanni" strongly recommends trained mental health professionals for those facing issues needing counseling.

Tom Swanson
aka "Professor OB1 Kaswanni"

ACKNOWLEDGMENTS

When I first saw this little girl 60 years ago, I asked my dad her name. It was at Covenant Point some 54 years ago that we first connected. My dear wife of 47 years, Donna, has been a wonderful friend and traveling partner. Patiently proofreads everything I write, very often adding insightful additions. Proves true the one-liner, *"Happiness is being married to your best friend."* Thanks for your long years of love, friendship and encouragement.

This book would not be possible without the personal and professional support of Marilee Donivan at www.SunriseMountainBooks.com. Marilee has not only provided wisdom and support in writing and publishing, but has been a personal friend with unending friendship, love and encouragement.

Blowing Your Knows In Public offers many thanks to the original authors and contributors to life's on-going fascination with one-liners. You are part of a national treasure.

There was no limit to the professors I had at the **"One-Liner University."** Teacher in-services, coaching clinics, sermons, students, conversations, mom's wisdom, bulletins, grandpa's wink and wit, newsletters, restaurant placemats, billboards, reader boards, email copies, *Country* magazine, *The Reader's Digest*, and comics have all been instructors that helped produce the wit and wisdom gathered from, and for, the common folk. The internet has produced lists upon lists upon lists of one-liners. Many times a one-liner was written on a little piece of paper and given to me.

A great source for my one-liner collection has been 35 years of high school yearbooks. I loved to see the one-liners each student chose, often showing the personality of the student.

The one-liner phenomenon has become the repository of the "wisdom of common man." One-liners often are used as commonly as words. It has become a way that many people think. Sincere thanks go to all the original authors and to all the folks who keep their wisdom and insights available, alive, and helpful.

Congratulations!

You have been accepted into

The School of Hard Knocks

Ph.D. Program
Wisdom Apprentice

All Fees Waived
Effective immediately!

Authorized by "**Professor OB1 Kaswanni**"

From Smart...

The early bird gets the worm, but the second mouse gets the cheese. ***Steven Wright**

It's not that I'm so smart, it's just that I stay with problems longer. ***Albert Einstein**

Whatever you do in life, surround yourself with smart people who'll argue with you. ***John Wooden**

I'm not the smartest fellow in the world, but I can sure pick smart colleagues. ***Franklin D. Roosevelt**

I hate to be smart. ***Paulo Coelho**

You learn how to be book smart in school, but you better not forget that you also need to be street smart. *** Harvey Mackay**

Smartness runs in my family. When I went to school I was so smart my teacher was in my class for five years. ***Gracie Allen**

You have to be smart. The easy days are over. ***Robert Kiyosaki**

Working hard and working smart sometimes can be two different things. ***Byron Dorgan**

Half of being smart is knowing what you are dumb about. *** Solomon Short**

Be smart, but never show it. ***Louis B. Mayer**

This life is a test—it is only a test. If it had been an actual life, you would have received further instructions on where to go and what to do.

...To Wise

Be as smart as you can, but remember that it is always better to be wise than to be smart. *Alan Alda

A smart man makes a mistake, learns from it, and never makes that mistake again. But a wise man finds a smart man and learns from him how to avoid the mistake altogether. *Roy H. Williams

A smart man only believes half of what he hears, a wise man knows which half. *Jeff Cooper

I'm not smart, but I like to observe. Millions saw the apple fall, but Newton was the one who asked why.
* William Hazlitt

Smart people are a dime a dozen. What matters is the ability to think different... to think out of the box.
* Walter Isaacson

We shall not grow wiser before we learn that much that we have done was very foolish. * F. A. Hayek

Criticism is easy; achievement is more difficult.
* Winston Churchill

Knowledge speaks, but wisdom listens. *Jimi Hendrix

Common sense is not so common. *Jessica Truman

You can tell whether a man is clever by his answers. You can tell whether a man is wise by his questions.
* Mahfouz Naguib

God gave us mouths that close and ears that don't ~that should tell us something.

* www.brainyquote.com

Coffee Break!

Laughter is an instant vacation.

Morning has broken—my coffee has spoken!

This is the earliest I have ever been late!

I like my coffee handed to me!

**If you don't pay your exorcist
you can get repossessed.**

**Everybody should believe in something.
I believe I'll have another coffee.**

**A dentist and a manicurist married.
They fought tooth and nail.**

Laughter is a tranquilizer with no side effects.

Is It OK To Blow Your "Knows" In Public?

Congratulations! You are already a veteran, experienced, and certified "Knows Blower!"

First of all, for every day of your life, so far, you have been *blowing your knows* in public. Everything you think, feel, do or say starts with what you *know*. All of your thoughts, feelings, actions, and values work together as you make decisions to daily live out your life.

Wherever you are, be all there!

Hopefully you have given yourself permission to take on a more and more assertive responsibility to lead your life. You can start today to be more purposeful and intent on making your life better moment by moment, day by day.

How many times have you been told to "wake up, wise up, heads up, or as we say in Swedish, "Tyst—(shut up!)" Every airplane pilot understands "nose up!" So, the new mantra for all us knows blowers is… "Knows Up!" Moving on from smart to wise will always be a moment to "knows up!"

"Knows Up!" Become incredibly excited! This is your personal Emancipation Proclamation. You are free to change masters and enroll in the *Wisdom Apprentice Program*. You are not obligated to be controlled by those negative voices demanding *you* adjust to *their* viewpoints. Only the best of wisdom is your future.

Wisdom will be a tremendous source of joy and fulfillment. You will celebrate the "best" life has to offer. You will begin to look forward and anticipate a better new day. Your "New Day's Resolutions" will empower your continued journey toward wisdom.

The wise know their "no's!"

When considering transforming from "smart to wise," consider the billions spent on advertising. Their research has convinced them the buying public will spend on cosmetics, stylish clothes, weight loss, body building, cosmetic surgery and countless other ways to help the consumer "look better."

One way of looking at that reality is that all the fancy wrapping on the gift package does not add value to the gift in the box. While looking good has some benefit to every individual, adding value to your wisdom, character, and effective people skills benefit you and everyone with whom you relate.

***People don't care how much you know
until they know how much you care.***

Blowing Your Knows In Public will attempt to clarify
the value and benefit of "smart." Smart is the ability to
gather and use information and skills. Like a smooth
running, powerful motor, smart needs an operator to
maximize the motor's benefit.

The goal will be for you to "purpose to pursue wisdom"
every day as you live your life going forward. Purpose to
be assertive in becoming an honor student in the school of
wisdom.

Wisdom focuses on the bigger picture of life, the things
in life that add value, beauty, and benefits to everyone. The
wisdom of the ages is the proven principles of a worthy
life, where smart are the practices, and which correctly and
effectively used can help wisdom and success occur.

Purpose to make wisdom your new master, and smart
his loyal effective servant. Just like putting the cart in front
of the horse, wisdom must be in charge.

My problem is that I am educated beyond my intelligence.

By far, the most important part of "blowing your
knows" is your self-talk. All of your knows come together,
and work together as you talk and tell yourself how that
process is unfolding daily. Carefully monitoring and
evaluating your self-talk is paramount if you want to start
and keep moving "from smart to wise!"

One of the first classes you took in Mommy School was
"Manners 101." Bet one of the first was, "Don't pick your

nose!" A high priority lesson was on how to blow your nose in public using good manners. It was part of the "do's and don't" curriculum.

The next time you have to sneeze, go ahead and try to stop yourself. How long can you endure a miserably stuffed nose without blowing it? At some point blowing your nose is not an option, but a must. Your education in the "School of Hard Knocks" continues. *You will blow your nose, and blow your knows!*

Ask "why" until you understand.

How well have your figured out this game called life? Are you stuck "Boldly Going Nowhere?" Many times you must have felt frustrated that you have had to learn the rules of the game of life completely on your own. In reality, that process is an unending, life-long process. You are now challenged to move on *"from smart to wise."*

Blowing Your Knows In Public will attempt to help you think through your process of figuring life out. Expect more questions than answers. My answers will probably not fit all your questions. Remember it is *your* life to live.

Things happen because someone makes them happen.

Knows Up! Your journey so far has been full of lessons learned, both on the positive and negative sides. Realistically we often learn most effectively in the hard times, where we are forced to come up with solutions. All that stuff contributes to what you know.

How did you come to know all the stuff you know? The more you reflect on that question, the more amazed you will be at your brain's ability to input, process, retain, recall and use the wide variety of knowledge you have acquired.

A prudent question is one half of wisdom.

When was the wake up call in your life? When did you become aware that you had to start figuring out this phenomenon called life? When did you realize that you had to assume responsibility to drive your own life? Are you continuing to move "from smart to wise?"

At some point in life, I bet you came to the conclusion that a lot of your "knows" were useless. Somehow you were snookered to think that stuff was valuable and important. Professor Experience taught you many valuable lessons.

Is everything you can learn really worth knowing?

Hopefully, you also came to realize you had a huge void of needing something wise and beneficial to guide your journey forward. At that point you started to grow up. The process of living forward wisely demands you are continually getting prepared for the next upcoming, challenging journey.

Another huge lesson of life is the absolute benefit of unlearning. A lot of stuff you have lodged some in your brain is just taking up valuable space. Whether you call it spring house cleaning, emptying your trash bin, or just plain "flush it," you will be greatly encouraged by getting rid of those burdens and "moving on."

Difficulty shows what you are made of.

A lesson I hope you have mastered is the foolishness of the "quick fix" or the "easy fix." It is impossible for me to know where you will find your starting point. As a student, wise application of these questions and considerations is a must. *You* must apply any and all instruction to your personal journey.

Knows Up! Reflecting on life, now you must effectively put your improving "knows" into practice. This will determine the quality of your life. *"From Smart To Wise"* requires that you must live going forward. Your best chance at success is the wise applications of solid thinking, day to day to day.

The smarter I think, the luckier I become!

Doing demands reflection and decisions that you are implementing those things based on proven, wise insights. Would you expect success to come from stupidity and foolishness? You will be challenged to do a little mental house cleaning, dumping into the trash bin, or "flushing it!"

Life is always moving onward and forward, but are you? Practically, if you continue being alive, that requires living out each new day. *Blowing Your Knows In Public* believes you can develop your skills at living more strategically.

It will be a huge, long-term benefit to learn to move *From Smart to Wise*. This paradigm, or theme, will run all the way through the book. My hope is that you will come to realize this life- changing benefit. Your self-talk will significantly mature.

Reality has a way of defining itself!

Reality has the final say in life, but do you still like to fantasize confidently about your ability to avoid it, influence it, and coax it into making reality adjust to your point of view? In your day- dreaming and planning, do you often overlook that possibility? ("Stuff like that just won't happen to me.")

Now it's time to "cowboy up!" Help wisdom become your new wagon-master as you bring a new paradigm to your ongoing journey. You will become amazed at the improvement as you travel through life.

Knows Up! By taking careful inventory of your "knows" warehouse, eliminating the non-productive, building a list of how to improve your "knows," your future can optimize your success. You must acquire and master those "knows" that empower you to reach the top of your next mountain.

Keep reflecting on the benefits of moving and growing from smart to wise. A major concept is that your life will become less controlled by the "smarts" of others, and decidedly enhanced by your development of wise living.

I do whatever my Rice Krispies tell me to!

So welcome aboard! Keep on reading and reflecting. There are plenty of "turn outs" and "viewpoints" to stop for taking time to have a little chat with yourself. Speed-readers will benefit by taking the old fashioned, slow and easy approach. Like fine wine, wisdom is best developed slowly.

The process of acquiring wisdom is like what it takes to create anything of value. Artists, writers, speakers, athletes and everyone who performs or makes a product keep polishing and perfecting their craft. Reflection and study that become alive in your demonstration of wise living will take time but you will benefit greatly. You don't help the corn stalk grow by pulling on it.

It is best not to grit your teeth, pump your chest, or ramp up to the max in your attempt to acquire wisdom. Keep improving the use of your sense of sight and hearing to acquire ideas and information. Learn from your fellow man. Learn to enjoy the reflection part of the growing in wisdom process. When the light bulbs start to come on and you start to connect the dots, you will be rewarded by the blessings the wisdom process provides. And the blessings and payoffs will continue as you journey.

It is overrated that everything in life must be done in the active tense. Many passive tense moments can help refine, improve, and perfect the process. You don't have to go after everything valuable in life. Absorb the morning sunshine, be fascinated by the butterflies, catch some lightning bugs, laugh with your family and friends, sit and just listen, enjoy the wonderful free things of life. Wisdom has the magic of taking all the input and finessing everything into things better and beautiful. Don't miss out. Enjoy and give thanks.

The most important thing you do is what you do next!

Coffee Break!

Laughter is an instant vacation.

Carpe Coffeeo: Seize The Coffee!

Where does the white go when snow melts?

Pour the coffee, and back away slowly.

**Have you ever imagined a world
without hypothetical situations?**

**I can't even tie my shoes
before I've had my coffee.**

**Would you give your right arm
to be ambidextrous?**

*Laughter is a tranquilizer with no side
effects.*

Will You Quit Listening to the "Know-It-Alls?"

Really smart people have somewhat challenged and intimidated me. I grew up with some really smart kids. It was motivating to hang out with them. Looking back at many of their life stories, they would have greatly benefited from a little seasoning of wisdom.

How is it that all the "knows" somehow ended up stored in your brain? While gathering all those thoughts, feelings, and experiences, did you consciously evaluate and organize your collection as you went along. In reality, stuff comes at us so fast it would be an impossible task.

Listening is both an active and passive activity. You can tune in and intently focus as you listen, or the noise and voices of our culture are always "messaging" you. It is your responsibility to filter all the sources of information coming your way. The wise master the acceptance of every message.

> *Growing up in the upper peninsula of Michigan [yes, I'm a Yooper], our furnace was a monster that took up half our basement. The question of Santa Claus visiting our house led me down into our basement. If he really comes to our house, how is it possible for him to get down our chimney, climb out of that huge furnace and deliver the gifts? I was highly skeptical!*

Is one of your motivations to grow and move from smart to wise? Just like the right amount of the right seasonings change eating into dining, so it is with moving from smart to wise.

Is this the moment where you say to yourself, "Self, it's time for a little reorganizing and prioritizing"? All the clutter and confusion really impedes and disrupts clear thinking and efficient action. Another way to visualize your current status is you are packing a lot of useless rocks in your backpack. So…

Success is not determined by doing your best, but by doing whatever it takes.

It is normal to sense a feeling of paralysis or being "whelmed." Most likely overwhelmed. You also might magnify the problem. The sooner you calm down, focus on the task at hand, identify possible solutions and select your next steps, the sooner your journey can continue towards success.

Blowing Your Knows in Public will be asking you to keep checking a wide variety of topics. You will have to decide what to do with these freeloading squatters in your brain. If they are not helpful or beneficial, will you have the motivation, skills and fortitude to evict them?

Vision is best described as your personal view of a preferred future. The more clearly defined your vision, the easier it is to see if your thoughts and actions empower that vision.

Take a deep breath. It calms the mind.

Knows Up! Consider yourself becoming a trailblazer into your future. Like those old pioneers and cowboys you will have to be more and more self-reliant. You will have to travel light, often into unknown territory and face challenges many times a day. Very likely you will be making a new road.

We directed a summer camp where we chose the theme for the summer: "The Adventure Begins Where The Road Ends!" Those earliest adventurers often started by taking their first step out the front door. Everything was new and uncharted.

The Lord gave you two ends: one for sitting, one for thinking. Your success depends on which you use. "Heads you win / tails you lose!"

Often in these new and undefined situations you learn a lot the hard way. In school the lesson plans usually follow the established curriculum. Many important lessons in life are non-curricular! Get ready to get a real world education, even if you didn't sign up for the class. The "School of Hard Knocks" continues.

You will very quickly learn you are not traveling alone. While you might be the only one on your journey, you will come to realize you are not traveling all by yourself.

Your mind is full of negative traveling partners. Many of them are unruly, obnoxious, bad mannered, highly opinionated, loud and boisterous. If you haven't established your dominance, ready or not, they will be heard.

Don't look back—you are not going there!

Knows Up! You must immediately call their bluff. They are so full of themselves they perceive themselves above and beyond criticism. You will be temped to try and adjust their attitude, and straighten out their thinking. NOT! They are a hopeless case, far beyond redemption!

Start thinking smarter than harder!

In the six short "aha" sections to follow, we will identify and focus on your ability to deal with these very destructive thought patterns. You must master them in order to maintain your sanity, and to intelligently continue your journey toward success.

These meddling, mental troublemakers are delighted to be hassling your journey. That's where they are at their best, complaining, whining, blaming, and really enjoying the chaos. They couldn't be happier.

The know-it-all knows what to do until it happens to him.

Being a highly responsible person, you might be tempted by Professor Perfection to start blaming yourself. **Always be ready. Life always just happens.** We live in an imperfect world with an unlimited number of moving parts and forces. Nobody knows what lies ahead in every situation.

Life is. Adjust!

Your most valuable traveling partner is your "self-talk"! The secret to your success will be in controlling the voices in your head, organizing and collecting your thoughts in order to give yourself wise counsel and encouragement going on to solutions.

Someone has to take charge of the uncertainty and chaos in your present situation. Since it is your journey, you have the opportunity and responsibility to take charge. Now is the time!

When you're in it up to your ears, keep your mouth shut!

Self-talk and self-control are fantastic traveling partners, encourage them daily and welcome their input. As the "IF" poem by Rudyard Kipling says: "If you can keep your head while everyone else is losing theirs, and blaming it on you." Composure is really self-composure, something you have to control.

Shortly after college I ran into a book, *Bill Bradley, A Sense of Where You Are: Bill Bradley at Princeton,* by John McPhee. I honestly don't remember anything from the book except the title. It spoke volumes to me. It made me focus on my starting point.

Wisdom is what to do next: virtue is doing it.
David Starr Jordan

Knows Up! As you make plans to continue on, you are very capable of gathering the information, and considering the options for a successful journey. You must take your strong thoughts, execute dynamic action, and keep checking with honest evaluation as you move along.

The best way to predict the future is to create it.
Peter Drucker

Wisdom has been described as "skill at living." Experience is a very demanding professor. You will always get the test before the lesson. You are making very satisfactory progress. Remember, the class never ends; you just get better at living successfully.

Persistence is what makes the impossible possible,
the possible likely,
and the likely definite.
Robert Half

Should

Bacon & eggs:
Hens are involved, but pigs are committed.

As a youngster, I was baffled when an older man said, "I will not 'should' on myself!" It was a new thought and I had no reference point from which to respond. My journey through life had taught me well.

"Shoulds" are seeds planted in your mind that can become like noxious weeds; they spread and take over. They arrive unnoticed, often very innocently. They come from anywhere, and everywhere.

Just like addictions, increasingly they are in charge of your life. It seems like you are on automatic pilot, unable to take control. Recognizing this unwelcome intruder is your first step to recovery.

You should *(oops! Bad boy!)* Carefully choose some "shoulds" based on truth and wisdom. They must be under your control and used to remind yourself of things you deem as very important. They can become virtuous traveling companions on your journey to success.

Knows Up! You can evict the "shoulds" that have bullied their way into your life. Your willpower and self-talk can overpower that pesky annoyance. *"Cowboy Up!"* and take control on your journey to success.

Temptations are like tramps. Treat them kindly and they return, bringing others with them.

What If?

Don't audit life. Show up and make the most of it now.

Big thanks to Ken Olson for writing a most helpful book, *"The Art of Hanging Loose in an Uptight World."* There were many "aha" moments that really made sense in my life. One of them was a chapter on "What If."

How many times have you thought to yourself, "What if?" While it is a perfectly good question, it often takes up permanent residence in your mind. Then the frequency and volume keeps growing out of control.

It clicked in my mind that I had to learn to control the use of that little thought. It was not a thought to paralyze my thinking, but a quick check that I had done some brief reflecting. There is no end to the "what if" possibilities.

Planning and reflection on possibilities is one step of your action-step plan for success. Plan the work is the first step, and then you must work the plan. Professor What If wants to keep you wondering where he can continue to dominate.

Knows Up! You can plan, reflect, and then "move out!" You don't have to remain stuck in the "what if" phase of life.

What does it mean when a speaker looks at his watch? Absolutely nothing!

Not Fair!

To ignore the facts does not change the facts.

My grandson was not yet 2. Out of the blue, Josh looks at me like a prosecutor facing the jury, "Grandpa, that's not fair!" It doesn't take long for sharp little minds to figure life out!

The problem is life is not fair, whatever that means, and we get consumed trying to make it fair. Professor Not Fair is usually the most vocal, and destructive of those freeloaders residing in your mind. There will be no peace until he is evicted and silenced.

Life is: adjust! Life and reality have a way of defining itself. No matter how hard you moan, groan and complain, you must adjust and relate to your reality.

Concentrating on life being unfair is about as useful as making a budget to spent your $500 million lottery winning without buying a ticket. Trying to "fair up" an unfair world is an emotional sinkhole. If you're weary, and worn out, evict the unwanted Professor.

Knows Up! You can make significant progress making a solid game plan and putting it into action. You will feel refreshed without the Professor Not Fair always nagging you.

Life isn't fair, but it's still good.

Why Me?

What is, is!

One of the frequent responses to difficulties is a whiny "Why me?" Somehow many believe that they are immune from the unpleasant side of life. Some like the feeling so much, they keep listening to that destructive voice residing in their mind.

The question arises, who is in charge of your feelings and thinking? To your peril, keep listening to those negative voices. As someone once said, they are the "nit-picking nabobs of negativism."

To maximize your success you must challenge these negative voices, and replace them with encouraging wisdom. See them as unwelcome free loaders who have set up residence in your mind. Eviction notices are in order! Now!

Energizing your action plans requires wisdom, not immature spoiled sports. You need cheerleaders and consultants interested in your success. Everyone must be on the same game plan leading to achieving your goals.

Knows Up! Whether it is called spring house cleaning, or reformatting your hard drive, getting rid of the negatives in your life is always a positive. Now is the time: *when in doubt, throw them out!*

Whatever your season of life, attitude makes all the difference.

I Was Gunna, But...

Never put off until tomorrow what you can avoid entirely.

Good intentions are good, but! For some folks that's the end of the road. Who knows if their ideas and plans had value since they were never put to the test?

Paralysis by analysis is a phrase coined to describe the *"I was gunna, but"* crowd. Identifying the problem and fantasizing about solutions might be a valuable start. Unless these ideas pass the "put into action reality test," they get lost somewhere in our minds.

Your life must be lived in the real world of daily living. Progress or success will be determined by evaluating outcomes of your ideas. ***"The proof will be in the pudding!"***

Life is not for the timid. Challenges must be faced and problems solved. Stuff will keep coming at you awaiting your successful solutions and accomplishments.

Knows Up! Every morning adds to the drama of your life. Be assertive and energized about making everyday a WWAA Day: Way, Way Above Average!

Sometimes you have to take the test before you've finished studying.

The Good Old Days

The best is yet to come...

"Oh, for the good old days...." How many times have your heard that phrase, or more importantly, used that phrase? It's time for a little reflective perspective.

I hope your "good old days" contain many wonderful memories. It is a joy to remember, and relive pleasant thoughts and feelings from the past. Be thankful to all those who have contributed to your collection.

The temptation is to spend too much time reminiscing. Life goes on, and life must be lived in the present. You presently are making the next contributions to your "good old days."

I remind myself often, *"in two days, tomorrow will be yesterday,"* Life can only be lived in the "now." Past tense and future tense verbs won't cut it.

Knows Up! You can't fix the past, and the future has not arrived. Make today's focus today!

Overcome the bad days to enjoy the good days.

Coffee Break!

Laughter is an instant vacation.

"It's coffee o'clock!"

> Why do psychics have to ask
> you for your name?

Sleep is a symptom of caffeine deprivation.

> What would a chair look like if
> your knees bent the other way?

Given enough coffee, I could rule the world.

> If "con" is the opposite of "pro,"
> then what is the opposite of progress?

*Laughter is a tranquilizer with no side
effects.*

SECTION 2

Is It Time To Sign
"The Eviction Notice?"

Be forewarned and advised, a fringe group of "Occupy America" has secretly infiltrated and set up residence in your mind. These squatters are entirely settled in and fully operational. They have announced they now have the "home court advantage."

Be aware that they have unlimited resources and are energized to battle you at every point and issue. They have a vested interest in continuing their squatting, freeloading lifestyle at your expense.

In today's lingo, your hard drive has been corrupted. They are so sneaky that you have been unaware of their growing dominance of your everyday operating system.

Your happy-go-lucky enjoyment of the everyday pleasures of life has fueled their optimism.

Remember… with friends like these, who needs enemies?

Most of those who must be evicted are contaminated with the fatal disease of "hubris," or "hybris." Those with hubris are possessed by excessive pride and unlimited self-worth. They are blind, deaf, and dumb to your concerns and are totally self-absorbed. Since they truly believe they are infallible, you stand no chance of influencing their opinions.

These voices believe that there is no truth until they define it. Their input is above discussion or evaluation. It is your place to accept their opinions and give them your enthusiastic support.

***To succeed in politics, it is often necessary
to rise above your principles.***

You will often hear these voices from the crowd of celebrities, politicians, and higher academia. Since they reside in their own little world, they have formed a mutual admiration society. Be very glad you don't live in that world, rejoice in the wisdom of your being a part of the common man crowd.

***Two things are infinite—the universe
and human stupidity;
and I'm not sure about the universe.*** Albert Einstein

While you might be alarmed or surprised, they have taken advantage of your disregard of a poor virus awareness system. Life is so doggone daily for you. You didn't have time. Now you will have to deal with their well-entrenched reality.

Their arrogance makes it very plain that they feel entitled to continue living off your generosity without ever having to say thank you. They have defined the reality to which you will now have to adjust.

As you come to realize their presence, they have no regard for your thoughts and feelings. They live on a one-way street where everything is going their way. They have no interest in your success.

Let me propose the Kwitcher Solution: *"kwitcher whynin"* and *"kwitcher belyakin!"* Simply stop those negative behaviors that waste your emotional energy and sabotage your rational solutions. Focus on positive evaluation, check for best alternatives, and keep moving in a positive direction.

Realize everyone sees the world through their own eyes—you included. Is there anyone who better understands your reality? Humbly and strategically pursue your *best* interests. Marshal all your resources to empower your best choices.

Knows Up! Bad news can become good news! Recognition is your first step. Now they must become a target with your highest priority. This will become a major test of your wisdom and will power.

I used to think I was indecisive, now I am not so sure.

Now is the time for decisive and forceful action. The squatters are perfectly prepared and positioned. They already know your arguments and weak points. You are up against a most entrenched opponent.

You might be tempted to believe that all you have to do is to evict these freeloading squatters. This must be a major part of your action plan. As they are being evicted, you must be planting the positive ideas that will replace their residence.

Get rid of anything that isn't useful, beautiful, or joyful.

The empty space in your life left by evicting the occupiers must be filled with well-behaved, beneficial cheerleaders. If they aren't, you invite these tramps to move back in, often bringing with them even more obnoxious partners toward your destruction.

Now is not the time to be nice. These eviction notices will be met with very effective resistance. Withstanding such efforts in the past, they have become more permanently rooted in your mind.

Knows Up! You must realize that you are the judge, jury, and law enforcement officer in managing your mind. You are the sole owner of your mind. Show up! Serve notice! They will move out or be moved out immediately.

Experience is something you don't get until just after you need it.

Expect the world's best demonstration of childish whining and resistance. You must immediately demonstrate forceful resolve and determination. The question is, who will blink first? You are standing on the high ground, so battle on.

Diplomacy - the art of letting someone have your way.

Dr. Ken Olson in his 1974 book, *The Art of Hanging Loose in an Uptight World,* has a very effective image to empower you. Everyone has memories of your parents asking, "Did you remember to flush the toilet after you went potty?"

Ken suggests that sometimes in life, we just have to "flush it." We need to realize that is the best choice available to us. You have finished your business, it has no value, and the best thing is to flush it and move on!

Certain stuff in life you just have to flush!

Challenges and obstacles in life present us with us a stark reality that we must face. The "Occupy Crowd" in your mind celebrates. It presents them with a wonderful opportunity to create chaos in your life. If you listen carefully, you can probably hear them "yucking it up."

If you want to successfully move forward, you need to unload things that weigh you down. Your journey demands your best. Every day is a new test in your administration of your life.

Be the change you want to see in the world. Gandhi

Evict! You don't have any desire to waste time. You must be on your best game, not being dragged down. *Never be so busy chopping wood you don't take time to sharpen your axe.* It is always "game on."

Remember again, *in just two days, tomorrow will be yesterday.* You don't have time to waste. Don't give those you have evicted a second thought. You have higher priorities and nobler goals to accomplish. Power up! Power on!

Is your attitude worth catching?

Growing up as a sports nut, I kept hearing, "Follow-through!" Whether throwing a ball, hitting a tennis or golf ball, or executing an effective fake in football, the follow-through is super important.

The eviction of unwanted, destructive thoughts and behaviors must be one of the first steps to a preferred future. Sometimes you have to be the bad guy and ramrod the process.

There's one way to find out if a person is a hypocrite: Ask him. If he says no, he is!

The wise always take a big-picture view of their vision for success. They really do keep the main thing, the main thing. They are not sidetracked by the pompous shenanigans of these unruly and disruptive adolescents who never have matured.

Keep your eye on your prize. Being confident of your eviction action steps will definitely move you on to greater success. You are focused on your success, while they are focused on their success—at your expense. Celebrate, as you free yourself from that destructive burden.

Knows Up! You will be energized by your empty backpack, no longer packing those destructive free loaders. You will be packing energy bars of wisdom and insight to help you speed up your journey to success.

Forget

Forget—Choosing not to remember!

Forget is one sneaky dude. You most likely have already learned how sneaky he really is. He keeps slipping into your thoughts and conversation, usually unnoticed.

It is one of our most polished behaviors how we casually can justify our forgetting. Little kids can use it sincerely and get away with it. Successful adults have learned how to remember correctly and in a timely manner.

I challenged my grandson Josh about the definition of *forget*: "choosing not to remember." His reaction was an indication that he understood. That was reinforced a short time later with his comment, ***"Grandpa, I am choosing to remember!"***

Choosing to remember is a solid building block on your foundation of success. Details and information must be remembered and executed in a timely manner. Don't expect to forget your way to success!

Knows Up! You can develop helpful organizational strategies for success. Then, remembering to follow through will prove highly beneficial.

Remember—that way you won't forget!

Ought

Blessed are the flexible, for they can tie themselves in "oughts."

Isn't it easy to figure out and live someone else's life? I bet you have contemplated a few *"should and ought"* ideas for others. It is rather obvious to understand the solution to their situation.

"Oughts" are suggestions or expectations placed on us by society, others, or very often ourselves. In our creative, flexible moments, we often fool ourselves with our own "oughts." Some reflection is needed to keep, or dump, some of your "oughts."

Many of these "oughts" take up residence in your mind without your awareness. They slip in undetected through conversation, by reading or watching, and they start corrupting your hard drive. They take on a life of their own, and you keep paying the price.

Taking a hard calculating look at every "ought" idea in your life is very beneficial. It helps to sort through those time-wasting "oughts." Keep the few worth repeating and reinforcing; more importantly, find those that must be dumped or flushed.

Knows Up! You are in charge of your life and your operating system. You will feel and be empowered by cleaning out all the trash and clutter that is burdening your operational process.

The sooner you fall behind, the more time you'll have to catch up.

"Miserabling"

I can handle pain until it hurts.

How you talk to yourself is by far the most important thing you do. Your thoughts, values and feelings come together and provide instructions for your decisions and actions. Your "self talk" should be your highest priority.

As Scott Peck once concluded, "Life is difficult." With that starting point, what comes next? How you decide to respond will define who you are!

"Miserabling" is one of the behaviors you can identify by watching others. By words or body position, folks can demonstrate a downbeat, defeated behavior. They keep broadcasting that life is difficult and getting worse.

We all have been inspired by those who seem burdened and overwhelmed, but who, somehow, are also upbeat and battling their monsters. *"I complained when I had no shoes, until I met a man who had no feet."* Whatever those folks have, I want lots of it!

Knows Up! Each and every day you can count your blessings and refine your perspectives. Your self-talk, positive thoughts, and purposeful actions can keep building your success.

It's been Monday all week.

"Awfulizing"

Gravity always gets me down.

Do you feel as if life is always raining on your parade? Are you becoming a professional mumbler and grumbler? Do you think bad luck is the only luck you have?

Even the most optimistic folks have those days and moments where life seems to be ganging up on them. Everyone has events in life that are very hard and painful. Learning to cope, overcome, and get back on the positive side is a skill worth mastering.

"Awfulizers" get stuck in their difficulties and keep repeating that thought. Some use it to reinforce their belief that life really is out to get them. Some folks might need professional assistance to help turn that corner back to realistic optimism.

Accurate self-talk is your greatest skill. Moving from real disappointments and difficulties back to purposeful living is the goal. You have the responsibility and opportunity to move yourself in a positive direction.

Knows Up! You can develop those positive self-talk skills. Start today by focusing on becoming your own enlightened, positive encourager!

Some days you're the bug, some days you are the windshield.

Perfection

It's nice of me to see you.
The pleasure is all yours!

Professor Perfection is as bad as bad can get. He is the personification of the bully of bullies. This narcissistic phony is so full of himself it is a wonder anybody will let him stay around.

The professor has absolutely impossible standards for everyone else, with the exception of himself, of course. Perfection is unattainable, period! Yet this loudmouth constantly reminds you of your failures to perform perfectly.

Professor Perfection is a total fraud and utterly non-redeemable. He must be evicted. With friends like the professor, who needs enemies?

To have made it thus far in your life, you must have had lots of successes. While everyone is somewhat imperfect, many successes are meritorious and noteworthy. Go ahead, stiff the professor, and pat yourself on the back.

Knows Up! Rejoice at the realization that perfection is impossible. Celebrate your uniqueness and continue your steady contributions of making your life and the lives of others worth living.

To become perfect, live by the advice you give others!

Experts

***Conceit is a disease that makes everyone sick,
except the one who has it.***

Have you had the thrill of being able to play the "trump card" and thus be able to win the card game? There is something final about playing trump cards one after the other. Nobody can do anything about stopping you.

We often seek and quote "experts" like they were trump cards. By the power of their reputation and expertise, the argument's over. I win!

If only it were ever so easy. There are experts available on every possible side of any argument. Tragically, some experts accept bribes to provide false information.

Careful selection of valuable trusted information is always very worthwhile. Be suspect—marketing experts have polished their craft to get results. Perceived experts are often their best "trump card."

Knows Up! You can develop your own expertise on your own life. Intelligently seek wise counsel and information to keep building your successful future.

***Go ahead and keep trying!
A rank amateur built the Ark,
while professionals built the Titanic.***

Coffee Break!

Laughter is an instant vacation.

A morning without coffee is like sleep.

When God made mosquitoes,
did he make a mistake?

Be a coffee-drinking individual - espresso yourself!

When do you quit lying about your age
and start bragging about it?

Caffeine isn't a drug, it's a vitamin!

How much deeper would the ocean be
if sponges didn't grow in it?

Laughter is a tranquilizer with no side effects!

SECTION 3

What Have You Learned in the "School of Hard Knocks?"

Denial is more than just a river in Egypt. Are you ready to admit you are currently enrolled in the "School of Hard Knocks?" Even more so, are you ready to admit you're learning a ton of stuff? While some is trivial, some is very beneficial?

Remember watching TV commercials, especially before Christmas, and you knew you just had to have one of those toys, games or gadgets? You wrote to Santa Claus, bribed your parents, and did you ever luck out on Christmas morning. You got everything you wanted.

So, why didn't all those super fantastic toys work like they they did on TV? Why didn't they say something about the batteries not being included? Why didn't they say you had to assemble it? Reality is not always student friendly, but you never heard that on TV.

Knows Up! A great percentage of your "knows" came from your "School of Hard Knocks" learning. You have to learn a lot of the confusing stuff in life on your own. Events teach you lessons not available from the normal sources.

The biggest obstacle is between our ears.

The wisdom of the ages is summed up quite briefly: bad produces bad, good produces good. Common sense really is common. But notice how often folks think and live otherwise.

Do you keep banging your head against that proverbial wall, or are you developing the wisdom of insights? Is wisdom leading you to accept certain truths and reality? Do you keep moving on to areas where you can keep growing and succeeding?

"The only true wisdom is knowing that you know nothing."
Socrates

This truth was identified ages ago. The ancient philosophers, writers, poets, and judges developed foundational principles of wisdom. Common points of wisdom cross cultural and historical lines. The life of mankind forces us to deal with the reality of certain issues.

> *Calvin gets all dressed up to go outside on a cold winter day. He goes outside, keeps wiggling his nose, and then makes a profound statement, "You know it's cold when your boogers freeze!"*   Calvin and Hobbes

Wisdom keeps popping up in every age, fighting for its ongoing existence. In our computer age the phrase arose **GIGO: Garbage In, Garbage Out!** The computer's incredible ability to store huge amounts of data is based on the centuries-old principle, "bad produces bad, good produces good."

Knows Up! Are you developing and mastering that evaluative skill? What's trash and what's treasure? What is sizzle and what's substance? The quality of your future is greatly dependent on that skill.

When in doubt, throw it out!

Sitting here thinking and wondering about smart and wisdom being age appropriate? While talking and visiting with my grandsons, I'm most interested in what they share and like to talk about.

Last night we did a skit at a Young Life camp in Ukraine. Reflect on the "mommy lessons" for each grade:
On the first day of 1st grade my mommy said to me:
> 1st *grade: never, never, never wet your pants*
> 2nd *grade: don't suck your thumb*
> 3rd *grade: don't eat your crayons*
> 4th *grade: don't play with lipstick*
> 5th *grade: don't pick your nose*
> 6th *grade: don't flirt with boys*
> 7th *grade: don't chew tobacco*
> 8th *grade: what happened to your hair?*
> 9th *grade: don't pick your zits*
> 10th *grade: what happened to the car?*
> 11th *grade: what's that on your breath?*
> 12th *grade: you flunked what?*

Warning: Dates in Calendar are closer than they appear.

Are your memories organized by your years in school? Every grade has a file where the good, bad, fun, hard times got deposited. Very often, lessons—some smart, some wise—stay there for life.

It seems indicative to listen to the general conversation topics of folks of different ages. At every age, the topics change. Surprisingly, the topics seem to plateau where some get stuck at a certain level and are not interested in the more mature or challenging subjects.

Few women admit their age; few men act it.

High school reunions are very informative. The conversation topics, hair, dress styles, and general behaviors produce a gap that seems to widen with each reunion. Some folks seem to mature, grow up, and move on in life. Other folks seem stuck.

As a math teacher, I found it interesting to note how quickly and competitively some students mastered a concept and advanced in their knowledge and skills. Others struggled and, at some point, moved on. Some folks appeared to get frozen and chose to move on to other academic subjects.

Knowledge is like a garden;
if it is not cultivated, it cannot be harvested.

Knows Up! A secret of life is to strive mightily to master the "smarts" and "wise" of every age and season. Again, you can learn to unlearn and discard the foolishness and "used up stuff" of days and times gone by. Remember, you do continue to grow up.

Never judge someone by the opinion of others.

Snookered

Half the lies they tell you aren't true.
Yogi Berra

"You been had, sucker!" How many times have you felt that you have been duped into believing something that turns out not to be true? Welcome to the "Graduate School of Hard Knocks."

Most folks are honest, trusting and just plain, good folks. They speak the truth and trust others to do the same. But, be forewarned… some folks just ain't that way.

While you are always encouraged to believe in the best of others, wise folks have developed the sixth sense about truth and honesty. I'm sure you have it heard said, "If it sounds too good to be true, it probably is!" And yes, this does apply to you!

I have always believed it is a lot easier to stay out of trouble than to get out of trouble. You do control your "yes" or "no!" There is NO pressure to say yes to anyone or anything else.

Knows Up! There are folks very skilled in using and abusing you. They can try to convince you that something is in your best interest. The wise develop the skill of sensing mischief ahead of time.

They said I was gullible,
and I believed them.

Life's Tough!

Two wrongs are only the beginning.

Your self talk controls your life. As you live each day, processing what is coming at you, how you talk to yourself determines your future. Learning to give yourself wise counsel is the best gift you can give yourself.

It is most helpful to approach life with a realistic attitude. If you expect everyday to be a Happy Birthday party for you, or a Santa Claus visit every morning, expect to be disappointed. Life will bring you anything, everything, something, or nothing.

Life is so doggone daily! Every day brings a new day, waiting for you to live it successfully. Realistic expectation of overcoming, solving, and making good things happen is a sound, positive starting principle.

You have arrived at today with some degree of success. The wise do not beat themselves up with perfection. They are just like the batter stepping into the batter's box, thinking, "I'm going to hit that next pitch."

Knows Up! Keep talking to yourself in realistic terms. Accept the challenges and opportunities of the day. Expect the best out of yourself, making every day another step towards improvement.

Never take life too seriously.
Nobody gets out alive, anyway.

Critics

For every action
there is an equal and opposite criticism.

Growing up, I remember an old timer telling me, "The dogs will always be barking!" We can expect the same from critics. That is just what they do. The wise learn to separate the truth from the mumbling and grumbling.

Your expectations set up your outlook for each day. Your ability to filter all the incoming stuff is super-important. The quicker you sense "critic" the sooner you can intelligently process that input.

"What do you expect from a smokestack but a lot of hot air and pollution?" This is a good insight into the critic in your life. The wise do not let the critic determine their future responses.

The wise have developed the skill to use any and all input, both good and bad. They control how that input will be translated into beneficial self-talk, producing growth and improvement. It is a skill you can learn to maximize.

Knows Up! Learn to quickly identify any beneficial truth coming from the critic. Quickly turn that into positive self-talk, empowering your next action steps.

Frogs are lucky—they get to eat what bugs
them.

Narcissists

A self-made man? Yes,
and he worships his creator.

Have you ever had to spend a length of time with an "I, me, my" kind of person? You had better be a world-class listener, for they have lots to say. They really do feel you are entitled to benefit from *their* opinions.

What are your thoughts on the comment, "There are two kinds of folks who enter a room: the first says, "Here I am!" while the second group says, "Ah, there you are?" Narcissists are self- absorbed, full-of-themselves, kind of folk. Their world is a very small, self-centered existence.

Everyone can be confident and assertive. You are entitled to live your life by contributing your best to your success and to the benefit of others. Strength of character and positive contributions add to the success of everyone.

The wise develop the skills and insights to empower and assist others, not just to entertain, or bore them. Wisdom is centered on a beneficial attitude and contribution to benefit everyone. *"All of us are smarter than any one of us!"*

Knows Up! You are not in a contest to impress the world. The wise are blessed as a by-product of encouraging themselves and all whom they engage, to enjoy the community of successful folks.

The older I get, the better I was!

"Know-It-Alls"

According to my best recollection, I don't remember.

Are you impressed with folks who are really good at the game of Trivial Pursuit? Being somewhat a buff of trivia, I give them credit. Sometimes I get frustrated when I can't answer the question.

Did you catch the name of the game? Trivia! Trivia is all kinds of interesting and unassociated information. Trivia is what you might call the *stuff* that needs to be sorted and prioritized for its value.

The "know-it-all" knows the price of everything, but the value of nothing. Cliff Calvin on the Cheers TV show was known as what every bar has—the bar "know-it-all." John Ratzenberger auditioned for another role in the show, but convinced the producers that the "know-it-all" personality would be a perfect fit.

The wise have filtered out the trivia and inconsequential stuff and empowered their "knows." The lessons and knowledge that can be used as building blocks are properly arranged, ready for use. Trivial pursuit might be a good treat, but not the main course.

Knows Up! Go ahead and enjoy trivial pursuit, it is fun. Just remember the wise empower their "knows," the real stuff of success.

What other people think of you is none of your business.

Process

If you don't keep moving forward,
your bike will fall over.

Process is one of the most valuable skills of the wise. Process is how you move from smart to wise. Couple your self-talk with a systematic process and you have a powerful tool to become wise.

At present, your brain is full of your "knows." Imagine them as a huge pile of pick-up-sticks. All these sticks represent the lumber you could use in a valuable construction project.

Process is the strategy of putting all of it together. Breathe, walk, sleep, are a few of the process words of everyday life. Process is the ongoing, continuing activity of living.

Moving from "smart to wise" will give you ideas for maximizing the process. Taking what you know, evaluating, and organizing it according to value, identifying what you really need to learn, are a few of the process ideas. There will be no "quick fix;" that is not what process is all about.

Knows Up! You can figure it out. Just commit to the ongoing journey of moving from smart thinking to wise thinking. As Bob the Builder encourages kids, ***"You can do it! Yes, you can!"***

Whatever doesn't kill you
really does make you stronger.

Coffee Break!

Laughter is an instant vacation.

Coffee in England is just toasted milk.

A camel is a racehorse built by a committee.

I could smell myself awake with that coffee.

Don't wait for six strong men to take you to church.

I orchestrate my mornings to the tune of coffee.

Should you trust a stockbroker
who is married to a travel agent?

Laughter is a tranquilizer with no side effects.

Will What Got You Here Get You Where You Want to Go?

Since you are reading this, you have arrived at this point in your life. If you live long enough, you will keep getting older, arriving at each new day. Your yearly birthday indicates you are getting older. Is your "wisdom quotient" keeping pace with your age?

Growing old is mandatory. Growing up is optional!

My grandsons provide some memorable conversations. When they were younger, I would ask them about their birthday. They instantly responded. In jest I would ask them if they had passed their test so they could move on to the next year. I told them if they couldn't pass that test, NO next birthday.

Your evaluation in life starts with your expectations. How clearly can you state your expectations? Whether you have defined them or not, you subconsciously have a lot of thoughts and feelings about what you would like to see happen in your future.

Looking back or looking forward, your expectations play a big part in how you feel and think about life. The smart adjust quickly to the changing stuff of life, while the wise try to understand and strategize to keep improving life.

You have to make it through the day to enjoy the sunset.

One of the phrases I hated was when my parents, teachers, or coaches would comment on my efforts saying, "Not bad." What a stupid phrase. What was I supposed to take away from that comment?

Knows Up! Most folks approach life with a purpose of living and doing something well. Most want to learn and succeed. If someone is putting forth the effort, our response should include positive content, or insight and instruction for improvement.

> My grandson Josh started playing youth baseball. He would step into the batter's box awaiting the pitch. Most of the time he would step away, waiting for the umpire to call the pitch a ball. He wanted to get a walk instead of a hit. The next time he came to our cabin in the mountains I was ready for him. I had 2 buckets of plastic balls and a plastic bat. I told Josh he was to hit every pitch, no matter where it was. He improved rapidly.

The lesson was that hitting was an action, something you do. Your attitude is to be a hitter. He has become a very good hitter. He learned you would never become a hitter until you swing the bat.

Mistakes are proof that you are trying.

Reflect on what got you to today. Today you are a sum total of your thoughts, actions, choices and reactions. You must have done enough correctly to arrive at today.

Let's reflect on the word *enough*. How do you know when you have learned enough? When is your effort "good enough?" Do you ever arrive at "enough?"

Your answer defines your understanding and attitude of your expectations. The perfectionist is never satisfied and beats himself up. Some folks accept "good enough" and adjust life to "that's just the way it is." The wise see life as a journey towards better and better outcomes.

When you go driving, do you wander aimlessly until you somehow find your destination? Most likely you find out how to reach your destination before you get behind the wheel.

Knows Up! The wise know life keeps increasing the knowledge and skill level to cope with the responsibility and possibilities life brings. Yes, you will need new ideas and skills that get you to where you want to go. Otherwise, don't complain about your situation.

> Dog Missing: Small dog, no tail, missing one leg, blind in one eye. Responds to the name, Lucky.

So, how do you look at your life? Are you stuck at "good enough," or are you striving to keep moving onward, upward, and outward? Do you think you will need to be lucky to succeed?

Alter your life by altering your attitude.

The greatest factor in getting you to where you want to go will be your ongoing self-talk. Keep encouraging yourself, becoming your best cheerleader. Keep your eye on the prize, taking one step at a time.

Smart is often focused on the short term, interesting and entertaining stuff. Smart likes to sightsee along the trip. Like the rabbit, he often is off in the buckwheat, chasing the new and distracting stuff.

Wise is focused on quality, long-term lessons of life. Wise is more like the turtle, plodding purposefully along, heading toward the finish line. Slow and steady will win the race.

Be the living expression
of God's kindness.
Mother Teresa

Knows Up! You can get to where you want to end up. You are constantly preparing yourself to become everything you will need to succeed. Realizing your need to keep moving from smart to wise will empower the process. You are right on track. *The winners are determined at the finish line.* Be proud to be a turtle!

Bigger isn't always better. Better is better!
Coach Chris Peterson, Boise State Football

So, congratulations and be thankful for what got you to today. All those skills and character traits, along with your "knows" have successfully helped you arrive at today.

Just like an automobile or so many things you own, maintenance and repair come with operating and owning. Isn't it fun when things break, wear out or die? The stuff that got you here might not be around when your future arrives early and unannounced.

Thinking back on my life I remember rotary phones, my childhood phone number 534, going through the operator, a manual typewriter, a slide rule in physics class, my dad's 13-key mechanical adding machine (state of the art for its day), phonograph became hi-fi became stereo records, cassettes, 8-track, reminding my that one must keep updating and adjusting to the best life keeps bringing your way.

Life is what happens on your way to somewhere else!

In the midst of constant change, sometime for the better, sometimes for the worse, wisdom usually changes very slowly. The wisdom of the ages has been found tried and true, not influenced by the newfangled upstarts making a lot of noise.

Wisdom provides comfort and assurance. Rest confident in your established understandings of the best you have determined. As my dad encouraged me, "Be true to the best you know." It has provided wise counsel all my life. Big thanks, Les!

Knows Up! Be careful about instantly on the newest bandwagon coming through town. Just like the "snake-oil" in the early days of America, learn to sort the sizzle from the substance. Buyer's Remorse has proven to be a nasty professor.

A fool and his money are soon parted!

And so the adventure continues. Keep juggling the two parts of life: where you are going, and how you are getting there. Wisdom keeps refining the decision-making and execution process. Here's hoping your journey is benefitting from lessons learned.

Continue being excited about those new creations, inventions, and solutions that really do bring great benefit to life. We do live in a changing world. Wisdom will continue to provide effective counsel.

Identify your problems,
but give your power and energy to solutions.

Knows Up! As you celebrate your safe arrival at today, anticipate the ups and downs of your continued journey. What will get you to your next destination will need to be the best of your fresh and new problem-solving and execution skills. Be grateful and befriend wisdom.

If it's not one thing, it's another. Some days it's both!

Look Back

Sometimes you get,
and sometimes you get got.

Better start thinking again if you are living in your rear view mirror. It's very tempting to stay stuck with past success, or failure. If you are going forward in your life, it is imperative to focus on what's ahead.

Hopefully you have a treasure trove of lessons learned as you are looking back. That should bring you great encouragement. You continue succeeding, while overcoming past mistakes. You are becoming a serious problem solver ☺!

Looking back is the boot camp and training ground for your next assault on success. You have been toughened up and are now in shape for the next monster you must defeat. Be thankful for lessons learned.

Continue to empower your "new day's resolutions!" As you approach today, expect new challenges to submit to your will and problem solving expertise. A new day brings new obstacles and opportunities.

Knows Up! You are getting better every day at dealing with the stuff you have successfully mastered looking back. Now you are looking forward to the next lessons to be learned.

Every path has a few puddles.

Look Forward

Hoping ain't coping!

Anticipate! What starts running through your mind? My hope is that there are positive thoughts about a better and better future.

Many times we are encouraged to pursue our dreams. Please be cautioned about the fantasy of living in your dream world. Far to often, one gets stuck there and never gets back to reality.

It would be far better to start defining your vision of your preferred future, and begin making a list of action steps to move forward. Better to start building than continue dreaming. ***"Plan the work, then work the plan!"***

Things get done because someone actually does them. Dreams reside somewhere back in your mind. To become of value, those dreams need to be defined and brought to reality by focused, determined work!

Knows Up! Today can be the day you adjust your plans and start executing your thinking and actions to begin *building* your future. Specific, definable effort will begin turning your dreams into reality.

Plan ahead.
It wasn't raining when Noah built the ark!

Look Inside

No matter where you go, there you are.

Some folk look everywhere for the secret of success except where it really resides. The secret is already firmly established and has set up permanent residence. The secret is alive and well dwelling within *You!*

Part of everyone's problem is that there are other jerks that have set up residence. All of us need to evict the negative freeloaders that cause disruption and chaos. We also must give special attention and consideration to wise and encouraging residents.

A former vice president often used the phrase: "the nitpicking nabobs of negativism." That perfectly describes those residents that have a lot of fun making destructive comments about everything in your life. Expect ongoing turmoil unless you evict them now!

Because of the loud, rude noise made by your internal enemies, the voices of wisdom, instruction, and encouragement often go unheard. Start tuning into those voices that are ready and very capable of helping you succeed. As my dad would say, "Be true to the best you know."

Knows Up! A little eviction and housecleaning will provide tremendous help. You will be blessed with the helpful voices of wisdom and encouragement already in residence.

I hear voices in my head
that don't speak my language.

Look Around

Half the people out there are below average.

It would be best to be very careful when you start looking around. Expect to see anything and everything. But be encouraged, you can find the excellent and commendable. *Just because something isn't wrong, doesn't make it right.*

You must really sharpen your evaluating skills when looking around. You must be ruthless in discarding the junk and keeping the treasure.

Discriminate used to be a very good word. Political correctness has destroyed its reputation. Still, you must be able to diagnosis the quality and value of everything and everyone.

There are many excellent ideas and models that can bring tremendous value and wisdom to your life. Likewise, there is real trash and disaster awaiting your poor choices. Just as in medicine and computers, the viruses of life are lurking. *Beware!*

Some folks live like the turtle, stuck and existing inside their shell. Intelligent pursuit into the fantastic world around you is a potential gold mine of information and wisdom. You must know the real thing, and avoid the "fool's gold".

Knows Up! What you are looking for to empower your journey toward success awaits you "out there." Continue to sharpen your evaluating and decision-making skills to enhance your success.

If something's wrong, something's wrong!

Look Out!

Loud doesn't make them right.

"Look out" is a skill you must master. Life always has a way of coming at you that is often surprising and unexpected. Don't panic or be possessed, but always be ready for anything.

My college basketball coach Royner Greene said the best players could see without looking. He called it "split vision." Having the skill of 360-degree vision is extremely valuable.

Clueless is a way to sometimes describe our situation. Either we are unaware or uninformed. Life sometimes plays "gotcha" with us.

Hopefully your professor in the School of Hard Knocks has taught you lessons to sharpen your awareness. A keen sense of what is happening around you will keep you on your toes. An effective game plan and effective personal road map will help you anticipate.

Knows Up! You are getting better about being ahead of those "look out" moments. When life surprises you, you are mastering your problem-solving skills.

Hang on tight.

Look Above

The Bible that is falling apart
usually belongs to someone who is not.

Bob Stromberg's song has a line, "Are you one of those people who don't need nobody else?" It really got me thinking. "Self-reliant" is the motto of the world. You are the master of your fate.

Try standing in a bucket, pick up the handle, and lift yourself off the ground. While self-reliance is a noble trait, as humans we are limited. Balancing ego and humility is a valuable skill.

Pascal said we have a God-shaped vacuum in our lives. Before our arrival in this life, and after our departure, self-reliance is a myth. It really will make a difference in your life to figure that out.

Jesus Christ claimed to be "God-in-a-Bod!" Jesus claimed to be God in human form, and that He came to teach and to redeem mankind. Was he a liar, a lunatic, or actually the Lord and Savior he claimed to be?

Knows Up! God's Word and the Holy Spirit are ready, willing, and able to help you come to a mature understanding. Understanding this really will become a blessing to you in this world, and the next!

The purpose of life is not to be happy,
but to matter.

 Coffee Break!

Laughter is an instant vacation.

Serious coffee - so strong it wakes up the neighbors.

I wondered why the baseball was getting bigger.
Then it hit me. Steven Wright

Coffee is a hug in a cup.

Quotes found on the Internet are not always accurate.
Abraham Lincoln

My blood type is Folgers.

Whatever happened to preparations A through G?
Steven Wright

Laughter is a tranquilizer with no side effects.

Section 5

Does Waiting Work?

So, did waiting help your birthday arrive sooner? Can you make some kind of a secret agreement for Santa Claus to come earlier and more frequently? Ask any mother-to-be if waiting for the last of the nine months for the baby to arrive made it happen any sooner.

Anticipation is often the greater part of the experience. Sometimes waiting and anticipating is a real pain. Why can't it just happen sooner? I'm already tired of waiting.

Ask a little kid if waiting is any fun. Nothing good happens when you have to wait. Wait, wait, wait......

"Time marches on!" And so it does, day after day, quite predictably. Wisdom certainly does not need to be complicated.

Understanding the major operational systems of life is valuable. So how do we benefit from waiting?

The difference between ignorance and apathy?
I don't know and I don't care!

Expect to do your fair share of waiting, or even more so. While waiting is non-productive, we know it is real. Since waiting is a waste of time, how can you turn the bad into good?

Whether you work at it, or just let it happen, time will pass. I remember in college reminding myself, "*Time will pass; will you?*"

If your focus is to wait, you will be wasting time. If you choose to move on to accomplish a task needing completion, the time will continue to pass, and you have made your time count.

Do you wonder while you wander? Daydreaming, wondering, and wandering will definitely help time pass. But, once again, what positive thing will happen? *Do you count time, or make time count?* Are you turning waiting into a positive or a negative?

With a calendar, your days are numbered.

Waiting can be productive when it fits into a well-defined plan of action. While waiting for the crops to mature, the farmer has a year-long agenda of necessary and important tasks. Ask a successful farmer how much wait time he enjoys.

Time management wisdom understands the "wait" period has a purpose. Therefore just let it happen. Something will happen in a defined period of time. Let life happen, and fill the wait time with purposeful behaviors.

Rest, relaxation, and recreation can be a fantastic way to use wait time. "All work and no play makes Jack a dull boy," or so goes the saying. Since you can't play during work time, use some of your wait time to have some fun. But don't overdo it.

It's never too late to start--
which is why I'm putting it off until tomorrow.

Waiting for something, anything, nothing, or everything is very foolish. Your wait time must have a defined purpose. *Some folks wait for their ship to come in, while they have never left the port.* Waiting in the abstract will produce absolutely nothing.

The novelty of work wears off very quickly. *Work very quickly becomes so doggone daily.* It is quite normal to find yourself daydreaming and fantasizing about retirement. If you do have a meaningful job and career, you will agree with Kermit the Frog: *"Time's fun when you're having flies!"*

Ask any retiree if retirement seemed to seek up on them much faster than anticipated. We seldom have a true sense of the actual reality of the passing of time. *"Why do the days drag on, while the years fly by?"*

The old-timer was proud of his increasing number of years with each birthday. He was brought up short when he received a birthday

*card message. **"Birthdays are just like a roll
of toilet paper: they appear faster the closer
they are to the end of the roll!"***

The longer you live, the more birthdays you have! If
you keep getting up every morning, you will keep getting
older, approaching your retirement day, one day at a time.
If you wait long enough, one day you can celebrate.

I'm retired – goodbye tension, hello pension!

What financial stability will you bring to your
retirement? What hobbies, or beneficial activities will help
you enjoy your retirement? While waiting, what
preparations have you made for the greater enjoyment of
your retirement future? When you do retire, what will be
the goal of your new "waiting?" While some folks keep
looking forward to retirement, they forget to live today.

The trouble with retirement is you never get a day off.

Tomorrow usually arrives early and unannounced.
Waiting works. You don't have to work at it. It just
happens.

"Move it or lose it" is good advice for keeping
physically fit. Maintaining good health requires daily,
intelligent investment in the right things. Try to make up
your one-liner about productive behaviors to produce
reasons to celebrate the end of your waiting.

So, does waiting work? In reality waiting really does
work—but only if *you* do!

***I always start my diet on the same day...
tomorrow.***

Waiting

Hurry up and wait!

What is your favorite childhood waiting memory? What were you so impatient about? What did you learn by waiting?

Welcome to the real world of reality. It seems we spend far too much time waiting. The older we get, we still feel frustrated and impatient while waiting.

Remember the little kid in *The Christmas Story* who was eagerly waiting for his "Little Orphan Annie Secret Decoder Ring." Turned out to be a lousy commercial. Waiting produced another kind of disappointment.

Waiting is just a part of the process for the wise. It goes with the ebb and flow of life. It is part of the price one pays for realistic living.

Knows Up! You can learn to be a relaxed, patient waiter. Waiting impatiently, without purposeful and productive behaviors, is a waste of valuable time for the wise.

**If you learn to wait a little faster,
things will happen faster!**

Waffling

I have not yet begun to procrastinate!

Has your indecision ever led to indigestion? Have you learned, *"Not to decide, IS to decide"?* Seems like "you're dammed if you do, and dammed if you don't!"

Where does the impression and pressure come from to make a decision? To make a decision is a choice you make. Putting everything in its proper perspective is a skill of the wise.

Urgency is a pressure you put on yourself. Wise anticipation of upcoming reality is a developed gift of the wise. They have learned to keep aiming high down the road of life.

Certainty in decision-making takes time, just like mastering that skill. The wise understand the wisdom of letting time mellow the process. Rushing the process creates undesired results just like trying to rush the time it takes to make fine wine.

Knows Up! Learn to enjoy the lessons learned from the decision-making process. It truly does make the present and the future more enjoyable.

I am at one with my duality.

Wandering

Nostalgia isn't what it used to be.

Have you ever heard the "nibble theory" of how grazing animals get lost? While eating, they keep their heads down, moving from one clump of grass to another. When they finally lift their heads, their first thought often is, "Where am I?"

So is wandering good or bad? The wise seldom think in terms of "either/or" but usually in terms of "both/and." Wandering is a perfect example.

Wandering takes you to places and thoughts you might not otherwise experience. Pleasant surprises, or impromptu lessons can come from your wanderings. You can always count on an interesting trip, full of surprises.

Wandering, sometime understood as "daydreaming," is a mystery. How often do you get lost in daydreaming? While it can be a waste of time, it often produces solutions with "free association" thinking time.

Knows Up! Enjoy the benefits of mental and physical wanderings. The wise have mastered the "both/and" uses of wandering.

Am I ambivalent? Well, yes and no.

Will Power!

Lead me not into temptation
(I can find the way myself).

Are you the master of your "will power" or your "won't power"? Once again, neither is the master of every situation and event in life. The wise use selective application.

I have two dear friends in Lowman, ID, Will and Wade. I often jest with them, "Where there's a Will, there's a Wade," or vice versa. They both demonstrate the value of both "will power" and "won't power."

Your willingness to accomplish positive things takes will power. The wise can make the decision to make it happen. ***"You get one of two things in life: results or excuses!"***

The wise understand the proper application of "won't power." It is a skill of the wise to say no to those things better left alone and avoided. The wise don't go looking for problems and trouble.

Knows Up! Empower both your "will" and "won't" power. It's just like the brake and the gas peddle; it takes both to arrive at your chosen destination.

You're just jealous because
the voices are talking to me.

For What?

Growing old beats the alternative—
dying young.

You might be asked the question, "What are you waiting for?" The wise not only have an answer, they have good reasons for their answer. The wise seem to know what, why, and the benefit of their waiting.

The wise build into the process all the questions and possible answers so that common sense is always on their side. They will not be fooled or snookered. They go with their eyes wide open, being right on top of every situation.

The waiting, waffling, and wandering have been tested by both will and won't power. They have defined and refined the playing fields and have learned the rules of the game. The wise are "large and in charge" of the process, not easily disturbed or sidetracked.

Knowing that "anticipation is often the greater part of experience," the wise are not only in the game, but also a few steps ahead in the game. One had better be a really sharp competitor to beat the wise at their own game. The wise come experience-tested!

Knows Up! You must also keep improving at the game of life. Being an excellent student has matured and helped you to master your growth from smart to wise.

He who gives only when asked
has waited too long.

Move It!

Moving on is often the best decision.

When traffic, or the crowd, is creating a problem, the authorities often send the word, "Move it, and move it now!" Sometimes patient waiting is a wise virtue. At some point more proactive action is needed.

The wise have developed a sense of proper timing. They have figured out the intelligent hunches. They come to realize that the time is now!

Having a realistic understanding of the process, and how events should be developing, provide great help to the wise. They have learned the intricacies of how progress is made. Evaluation is a normal, developed part of their thinking, always keeping them on top of the details.

Maybe you have to cut your losses and move out and onward. Learning lessons, or identifying failure, leads to an effective back up plan. Motivation to improve the chances for success is imperative.

Knows Up! Successful projects take on a life of their own. By partnering with wisdom, your chances of satisfactory progress will be forthcoming.

Paralysis by analysis!

Coffee Break!

Laughter is an instant vacation.

Hand over the coffee and no one gets hurt!

Do the Alphabet song and Twinkle, Twinkle
Little Star have the same tune?

Instant human, just add coffee.

Ever stop to think and forget to start again?

Is coffee your daily grind?

What is the speed of dark?

(Bet you started singing the alphabet song.)

*Laughter is a tranquilizer with no side
effects.*

SECTION 6

Can Bad News Be Good News?

If it weren't for bad luck, I'd have no luck at all!

My guess is that everyone reading thus far is a serious veteran of "bad news." Some folks even get a "pin cushion complex" feeling that life is somehow always picking on them. Wisdom understands we do get sick, flat tires, plugged toilets, and stuff that breaks, but somehow life goes on.

The real news today is that "bad news" will continue, BUT…

Bad news can become good news!

Knows Up! Students of wisdom are students of life. The mysterious challenge of life continues as we identify problems and obstacles. Some folks think they are so wise and brilliant because they can identify and point out problems. They really are clueless unless they can provide insight and understanding on the solution side.

Some folks don't have a clue, they don't have a clue.

It might often appear bad news has its own personality. This character could be described as creative, clever, tricky, and foxy. Adversity seems to know our "hot buttons" and has written a personal "bad news" prescription for each of us.

It is my understanding and conclusion that most folks have a sincere desire to live and remain on the problem-solving side of life. The wise have become students with advanced degrees in optimistic, aggressive problem-solving. Unfortunately, the following seems far too true:

Every time I find the meaning of life, they change it.

We live in a continuously changing world. Lessons learned in one situation do not automatically apply in every other situation. While the basic principals apply, you must target the unique problem every time.

Laughter and a light-hearted spirit can help tremendously. The old Negro spiritual combined an optimistic spirit with deep religious faith to combat the "bad news" in the life of the Negro slaves.

While it might seem humorous to watch comical, but painful, things happening to others, it is a far different story when it applies to us.

This would be really funny if it weren't happening to me!

It will take a strong dose of serious fortitude to stay focused on improving your troubling situation. Wisdom guides a person through the hard part where a deep inner best is needed.

Wisdom understands the loneliness of personal reality. Sometimes you really are in it alone. You personally have to face your monsters, pay your individual price, and ride it out through the tough times.

Laugh and the whole class laughs with you;
but you stay after school alone!

Expect to vacillate and fluctuate between your personal highs and lows, ups and downs. You will often feel like your roller-coaster car is out of control. Will you ever arrive safely?

Knows Up! Keep your composure, target your problem with well-thought-out actions steps, work diligently, follow through, and watch your progress.

Frequently it will become a battle of wits and will power. Will you prevail? Will your action plan win the battle? As we say out West: "Cowboy Up!" It really is up to you and a few of your sidekicks.

"Plant your feet securely in the right spot. Then stand firm!" President Abraham Lincoln

Two words pack a punch when it comes to understanding the timeline of life. *Practices* are the daily details of getting successfully through the day. *Principles* are the values and wisdom that keep the days connected into a lifeline of valuable, purposeful living.

Smart folks are very interested in keeping up with the latest and greatest. They pursue the new, different, and unique. Gimmicks, gadgets, styles and fads keep life interesting. Books, movies, philosophies, and personalities keep conversation entertaining.

Wise folks are equally interested and curious about keeping current in life. But they add the wisdom of the ages to help put the new and fascinating into some kind of a proper perspective.

***Someday we'll look back on all this
and plow into a parked car.***

The world keeps coming at you day after day. It won't change. Your principled response provides the realistic understanding that stuff keeps coming your way, but you are a seasoned veteran of the surprises life brings you.

Knows Up! Yes, it might show up on your doorstep, appearing to be bad news. You can readily see through the disguise and instantly start thinking about your solutions. You know it takes lemons to make lemonade.

It is the perfect time for your self-talk and self-control seasoned with wisdom to win the day. The wise are not easily intimidated by the realities of life. The bad news motivates them toward solutions.

***If your mind goes blank,
don't forget to turn off the sound.***

Reality!

Today is tomorrow's yesterday!

Those old time bare-knuckle brawlers must have been really tough dudes. They instantly knew they were in for a real fight. Reality does have a way of defining itself.

Reality forces the issue. As life comes at us every day, good news cr bad news is easy to identify. There's no polish, no fluff, just the obvious.

One becomes wise and successful by taking a positive, problem-solving outlook at the newly defined reality. No fantasizing, blaming, or avoiding! Understand, define, and attack the problem, targeting on solutions.

The wise do not wear rose-colored glasses. They focus and hone in like a laser. Optimistic expectations are the driving force toward creative adjustments and solutions.

Knows Up! Reality-based problem solving is a learned behavior. You can choose to empower your self-talk to use the energy of wisdom as your ally.

**However good or bad a situation is,
it will change!**

Gut-Check!

There is no right way to do the wrong thing.

"Whoa, I didn't sign up for this!" It doesn't take long to realize your reality check just presented you with a monster. Professor Self-Doubt is screaming.

Looking back at the real heroes of history and faith, they somehow passed the "gut-check" given to them. One can wonder where their strength of character arose. It is inspiring stuff that heroes are made of, making them worthy of remembering.

Some bad news really will challenge you to the core of your being. You will have to dig deeper and be wiser than ever before. This time it is very serious, far beyond anything you have ever faced.

The same process of wise application is the goal. Focused strategies based on hard facts, wise action plans directed at the real problem, followed by constant monitoring will produce the best chances for success. No foolish experimenting. Only the best of everything is allowed this time.

Knows Up! Only fairy tales always have a happy ending. The wise always seek out the best in every situation; so, you must do the same.

My Reality Check bounced.

Perspective

Horse sense is what keeps horses from betting on people!

Who came up with the phrase, "Better take a second look?" What was the thinking behind that idea? It is the stuff that wisdom develops.

Perspective is the vantage point from which you observe life. Understanding the strengths and weakness of your observation point is very valuable. I've learned from the wisest folk I know when they ask me, "What am I missing? Help me out."

The wise always seek input from several points of view or perspectives. Often it only takes a word or thought to trigger another insight for the wise. The goal always is successful solutions.

"Swallowing your pride never gave anyone indigestion!" The wise are not egocentric and small-minded. The wise have a big picture viewpoint, proving helpful to others.

Knows Up! Jesus gave wise insight and counsel when he suggested it takes asking to receive, knocking to having doors open, and seeking in order to find. Wisdom is really quite simple: go looking, keep asking, be willing to learn, and don't be surprised when wisdom shows up smiling.

He who dies with the most toys, still dies!

Possible

Everywhere is within walking distance if you have enough time.

There is power in "possibility thinking." Only one option is seldom reality, and that would be very limiting. Flexibility is not only a benefit to your muscle tone, but also to your mental tone.

I remember chuckling when I first heard, ***"If your only tool is a hammer, you tend to see every challenge as a nail!"*** Other possible alternatives might be welcome. Pounding does not solve every problem.

Consider the tinkers of history. Many were the subject of ridicule and laughter. But who had the last laugh in the end?

Life is not always linear. Solutions often come in very roundabout and interesting ways. Maybe it wasn't such a crazy idea in the first place.

Knows Up! Your mental wanderings and creative scheming just might trigger the possibility that produces results. Empower your random access: think about *Alice In Wonderland* and her wild adventures.

I almost had a psychic girlfriend, but she left me before we met.
Steven Wright

Probable

Time is what keeps everything from happening at once.

Man, how I hated probability problems in math class! They fried my brain. Now I'm glad some gifted folks can, and like, to do them.

Just as the whole gambling industry is built on probability, so one can get valuable input from the problem-solving world. We all understand certain behaviors have a better chance of success. You will *never* win the lottery without buying a ticket.

The wise understand the uncertainty of risk. Even the best farmers can't control the weather. They take into consideration every factor that will improve their chances for success.

Intelligent evaluation of the input you can use to plan your actions is important, and valuable. Dictionaries don't come from an exploding print shop. Considering probable outcomes are vital to successful action planning.

Knows Up! You are getting smarter and wiser everyday. There is a good probability today is the day your step toward success occurs. Bet on it!

Lead, follow, or get out of the way!

Predictable

My prediction:
The team with the most points wins.

We are just about to land in Amsterdam, arriving from Minneapolis. By the way—right on time. Was that possible, probable, or predictable?

Mankind throughout history has been fascinated by fortune-tellers and prophets. There has been no shortage of prognosticators about the future. Have any of them ever been held accountable?

Being able to predict the future is a proverbial, unscratchable itch. Even in our unconscious thinking we play our hunches. We would like to think we could foretell the future.

While you might not be able to accurately predict every detail of your future, you can greatly influence the results. Guided by wisdom and intelligent planning, you really can make certain things happen. You and others can be blessed because you helped make the outcome better.

Knows Up! You can be doubly blessed. Enjoy seeing the creative problem-solving process make your life and other lives better.

Weather prediction for tonight: Dark!

Profitable

Forget those who don't belong in your future.

Just like a teakettle, I hope you are leaking steam! You do have the ability and opportunity to *know* that you can become an agent of change, helping make the bad better—maybe really good. The wise believe conscious effort can seriously impact the future.

Your former self would get sidetracked and delayed by those folks squatting in your mind. Congratulate yourself on their successful eviction. You are now reaping the rewards of "moving from smart to wise."

The wise keep reminding themselves and reinforcing the new insights into their expanded world of wisdom. Expect that your new attitude will keep on adding to your valuable "knows." Aren't you excited and encouraged?

Keep a watchful eye! You continue to be a prime target for the forces of mischief and evil. Having been evicted to somewhere else, they are looking for a new residence.

Knows Up! Maintain your wise application of a healthy lifestyle. You can be the sunshine that brightens your day and those you are traveling with on the same highway of life.

Walk your talk.

Coffee Break!

Laughter is an instant vacation.

On the eighth day God created coffee.

An agnostic, dyslexic insomniac: stays awake
contemplating the existence of Dog!

Retirement is one great big giant coffee break.

Never let a fool kiss you—or
let a kiss fool you.

Retirement: World's longest coffee break.

To do is to be [Descartes].
To be is to do [Voltaire].
Do be do be do [Frank Sinatra].

*Laughter is a tranquilizer with no side
effects.*

Can You Encourage Your Confidence?

Dr. Robert Stone was my Latin and Greek professor in college. He was a fantastic educator, making class interesting and relevant. We translated Winnie the Pooh, plus many one-liners from Latin to English. One that I remembered was, "There are as many opinions as men."

With a sincere desire to keep moving from smart to wise, how does one develop the confidence to choose wisely and move forward? So far, we have identified and processed some of the many over-opinioned voices clamoring for your attention. Can one develop the confidence to combat their volume?

Speak in such a way that others love to listen to you; listen in such a way that others love to speak to you.

Confidence is that calm, inner assurance that you are on the right track, going in the right direction. First of all, you must accept the personal opportunity, responsibility, and freedom life gives you to live according to your best choices and efforts.

Just as every other person is entitled to his or her own opinions, *so are you!* While peer pressure and political correctness bombard you to adjust to their views, you do not have to justify your choices. You are a big person living your own life.

When it comes to going after what you love in life, don't take "no" for an answer.

In the marketplace of ideas in a pluralistic society, you can seek out what you determine is the best for you. You can encourage yourself and "spur yourself on!" Wisdom provides great counsel and encouragement.

Don't squat with your spurs on!

Confidence is built on a wise foundation consisting of trust, belief, reliability, certitude, and assurance. Confidence is not some abstract phenomenon existing out there in never-never land. Properly understood, confidence must be self-confidence. That must become one of the major factors in your self-talk.

Wisdom counsels that you are on a constant journey to maximize your certainty. Your confidence must result and rest on reflection and your processing the best information.

Understanding the competing voices that will constantly challenge your confidence is very important. As Pogo once said, "We have met the enemy and he is us!" Do you believe smart and wise are basically the same? ***There are two theories about arguing with some folks—neither works.***

Smart has a significant lead in the "World's Greatest Imposter" contest. He continues to baffle, bamboozle, pontificate, and bluster his way to significant importance. A little reflection will unmask this fraud. Self-control is not his strong suit.

Smart has no criteria for credibility. You can be smart and skillful in an unlimited number of areas. Prisons are graduate schools for "bad-smarts." Crime, corruption, gambling, drugs, vandalism, and the list of being smart at the wrong things goes on and on.

Being smart at wrong and immoral things has no merit. There is nothing praiseworthy of being smart in all the areas that are destructive in the lives of people. Smart is easily identified as an evil actor and agitator.

You have the capacity to learn from your mistakes, and you will learn a lot today.

"Street smarts," on the other hand, are the living skills that have helped many folks survive in a very complex world. Living day to day, one paycheck away from becoming homeless, is a challenge that produces "street-smarts." Wisdom is skill at living, up and down the entire social ladder.

As you walk the streets of your daily journey, keep reminding yourself of your "do and don't" list. Speak directly and forcefully to those negative and distracting voices. You have adopted the *Kwitcher Solution*. Remind them they have no place in your life:

"Kwitcher Whynin!"   " Kwitcher Belyakin!"

Since you are constantly working the plan you have established for your successful future, you daily must empower each "do" you have as a target for each new day. Your "New Day's Resolutions" will keep you moving one step closer toward success.

Be content to act, and leave the talking to others.

Smart has a very valuable place in your life. When taken properly, smart can be very beneficial in gathering and processing information. When properly controlled, smart can be a genius at getting the data and information for the wise to properly process.

The wise have taken the best skills and reformed them to produce wise, beneficial, and meritorious results. All skills can be used for good or evil. The wise produce good for all concerned.

Knows Up! You can keep transitioning from smart to wise. Use your best wisdom to evaluate the results of "smart" behavior and keep choosing the best.

You can lead if you get the lead out!

Foundations of smart might include the abilities to know, understand, analyze, plan, do, and reflect. These tools in your smart tool kit are very beneficial. Keep working on smart, but remember the limitations, and place for smart.

Wisdom always maintains the role of a student, while it builds self-confidence. With serious reflection and evaluation, wisdom takes all the "smarts" and confidently modifies and refines the input. The results are saved on your "hard drive of life" as wisdom, ready to provide quickly available counsel in the future.

I took an IQ test—the results were negative.

Knows Up! You can count on the self-confidence of wisdom. Wisdom is no charlatan playing games with your mind. Wisdom can be trusted as one of your best friends.

Your self-confidence will need to be empowered daily with successful reinforcement and reminding. As you are traveling, wisdom needs your full support. The secret of wisdom is the daily application, thereby championing wisdom as a foundational operating principle in your life.

The more I want to get it done,
the less I call it work.

Optimism

Few defeats are fatal.

I'm typing this in the Minneapolis airport on our way to Young Life camp in Ukraine. Our group from Boise, Idaho has chosen a little camp chorus, *"Oh, the sun's coming up, it's a bright new day!"* as our theme song. Do you see each new day as a bright possibility?

Wise folks have chosen mental, emotional patterns or paradigms about living successfully. Optimism must be high on the list. A positive outlook on life greatly improves your getting up and facing every new day.

Your outlook and attitude is your foundation to problem solving. Knowing stuff happens preps you for reality. Optimists know life is challenging.

Optimism is *not* a fantasy, pie in the sky, everything will always be hunky-dory kind of thing. Optimists understand life can bring anything and everything possible their way. Optimists just take life as it happens, realistically looking for solutions and proactively working to make things better.

So, Knows Up! Plant your feet, face into the wind; indicate to life to "bring it on!" Anticipating anything and everything gives you a "ready, set, go" mentality. The expectation of every optimist is that they will embrace life's challenges so that their journey will lead to the best results possible.

For people who like peace and quiet: a phoneless cord.

Hope

Happiness depends on ourselves. Aristotle

Hope is one of the foundational realities of mankind. The will to keep getting up every day rests on man's belief that his life and efforts have meaning. I can influence the outcome of every day.

Hope validates human endeavor. Those who are able to make their individual and community lives better demonstrate their belief in hope. The results are determined or influenced by our intelligent efforts.

"Hope springs eternal," describes the heartbeat of the wise. Wise thought and action will produce benefits. Our intelligent efforts will improve the outcome.

Hope is an operational paradigm of man, both for now and eternity. Every religious philosophy advocates that behaviors and beliefs will influence eternal outcomes. Our efforts are based on belief in purpose and promise.

Knows Up! The wise search and seek for the best information on understanding life. As my dad, Les Swanson, taught me, "Be true to the best that you know!"

I played a great horse yesterday.
It took seven horses to beat him!

Effervescence

I hate fishing. I love catching.

Doesn't the song go something like, *"Tiny bubbles in the wine, make me happy make me feel fine?"* Would you be described as having a "bubbly" personality? I still have a childhood memory of Vernor's ginger ale with the fizz tickling my nose.

The wise have mastered the selective and controlled use of energy and enthusiasm. Nothing significant is ever accomplished without energy and enthusiasm. Remember when a gas company encouraged us to "put a tiger in your tank?"

Gasoline works well when used in a fine-tuned automobile engine. It is quite disastrous to toss it on an open fire. Undisciplined use of your personal energy is equally true.

The wise have learned to turn thoughts into insights into action steps that only will be accomplished by energetic action. They also have fine-tuned the delivery of enthusiasm in a focused timely manner. Success in many tasks requires a smooth delivery.

Knows Up! You can greatly enhance your success by mastering your emotions. Display your "knows" with calm, effective efficiency!

If people are trying to bring you down, it must mean you are above them.

Stability

I let my mind wander, and it never came back.

When I was growing up, Prudential Insurance had a marketing line, "Get a piece of the Rock!" Their marketing image was the Rock of Gibraltar, that massive landmark between the Atlantic Ocean and the Mediterranean Sea. Remember the Bible story about the wise man building his house upon the rock?

The wise have built their operating system on a solid foundation. In ancient Greek mythology, didn't Atlas say, "Give me a solid place to stand and I can lift the universe?" A solid foundation sure provides for safe, stable, lasting construction.

Instability leads to uncertainty, confusion, and chaos. Bad information, bad planning, and bad execution lead to bad outcomes. In computer lingo: ***GIGO: Garbage in, Garbage out!***

Stability must be a mark of every step in the wise "knowing" on their way to success. Learn to delete the garbage and download the "knows" that empower movement in a positive direction. Power up your stable operating system!

Knows Up! Turn possibility into probability with a focus on stability. Trust the wise, proven "knows" of success.

*I've got to sit down
and figure out where I stand.*

Persistence

Hard work pays off in the future.
Laziness pays off now.

Things get done when someone gets them done. Time is not the main determinant. The successful completion of the project is the goal.

I love Thomas Edison's comment on making the light bulb. It went something like "I've learned 10,000 ways to NOT make a light bulb." Talk about persistence.

I wish I could remember way back when an older friend told me the secret of success: "Behave like the stamp. Stick to it until your job is done." Think "stickabilty."

The wise have mastered the process of persistence. They keep applying the best thoughts with dynamic action, monitored with honest assessment. Persistence is the dynamic action empowering all parts of success.

Knows Up! Persistence can be employed when your "knows" understands that "the winners are determined at the finish line!" Remember to keep your eye on the prize and finish strong!

Diplomacy: the art of letting someone have your way.

Smarts

The woodpecker is successful
because he continues to use his head.

So, how important are your smarts? While our focus talks a lot about wisdom, does smart really have a place? A big part of wisdom is in knowing the value of smart.

My wife and I were so proud of our first car, a white VW bug with red interior. It was all we could afford as early-married folk. We came to realize our good gas mileage was a result of a very small engine.

Smart is like the motor in your mind. Folks can be smart in a wide variety of areas and skills, both good and bad. Be thankful that you are blessed with smarts.

Your smart vehicle needs a driver/operator. The more wisdom you develop and use will greatly empower your journey through life. Continue to use your smarts to maximize the development of your wisdom.

Knows Up! Your development of wisdom is very doable. Pursue the wisdom of the ages and apply wisdom to your life.

Why fit in when you were born to stand out!
Dr. Seuss

Coffee Break!

Laughter is an instant vacation.

A cup of coffee shared with a friend is
happiness tasted and time well spent.

If age is just a number,
can I get mine unlisted?

Coffee, the finest organic
suspension ever devised.

An optimist stays up until midnight
to see the New Year in.
A pessimist stays up to make
sure the old year leaves!

Drinking too much coffee can
cause a latte problems.

Why do we say something is out of whack?
What is a whack?

*Laughter is a tranquilizer with no side
effects.*

SECTION 8

Are You A Smart Aleck
or a Wise Guy?

Do you remember a classmate that was the class clown? Or was that you? Do you have the gift of quick wit, or the instant comeback? Do you remember someone who really did know almost everything?

> *You can always tell the smart aleck,*
> *but, you can't tell 'em much!*

During our growing up years, the challenge of learning, knowing, and everything in between strains almost everyone's brain. Looking back, I bet you think a lot of your school learning was a waste. All the trivia from your childhood was a lot of fun. Millions of folks watch "Jeopardy" every night.

> *Life's a rat race; it looks like the rats are winning!*

So what is the difference between smart and smart aleck? Is being a wise guy a compliment? Growing up in a competitive family and community, I really wanted to learn to impress others. I was interested in more than good grades.

> *The sign painters were proudly walking off the bridge. Their new sign said,* **"Do Not Feed The Sharks!"**
> *Approaching them, a local said, "What's with the new sign? We don't have any sharks around here!"*
> *The sign painter replied that the new sign would work a lot better than* **"No Jumping From The Bridge!"**

Smart and wise are both closely related to curiosity, desire, ambition, and motivation. Mankind must input everything needed to compete successfully. The philosophers argue whether we are born with an empty brain or a partially loaded brain.

Knows Up! The intensity needed to input, or download, all the necessary and desired information really does rest and depend on you. *Don't expect to win the lottery if you didn't buy a ticket.* You need to be your own personal ramrod, empowering your intellectual development.

The devil is in the details.

While a mechanic or carpenter needs a toolbox of the proper tools, your intellectual toolbox needs the right mix of smart and wise tools. You can only build with the tools you have mastered.

> *The caveman approached the hardware store cave. There was a group of folks wandering around near the entrance. The sign near the door said,* **"For Faster Service, Invent A Number!"**

Just like many occupations requiring a training period to learn the knowledge and develop the skills of the trade, so it is with wisdom. Your on the job training makes you a certified employee.

In life you really are on a life-long wisdom apprenticeship. To become truly wise you keep transforming your smarts into wise. Your youthful wit, wacky and tricky comments must become moderated into meaningful, wise perspectives on life.

Instead of always entertaining the crowd and looking for a laugh, you are transitioning into a friend who amazingly starts to sound like your wise and encouraging grandparents. When did that change begin? How did you move from smart to wise?

Invent your plausible deniability.

The smart are quick on their feet, able to talk themselves into and out of almost anything. The end justifies the means. The wise understand it is easier to stay out of trouble than to try and talk their way out of trouble.

There really is a place for fun, good humor, laughter, and entertainment. Life provides plenty of material for us to laugh. The best comedians can make us laugh at our human condition and experiences.

Be careful of your thoughts—
they may become words at any moment.

Knows Up! A very significant part of this change from smart to wise is your personal change of perspective. You desire to move on. The Bible talks about putting away childish things as you grow older.

My dear Pastor David Roper sums up the process in both the title and the writings in his book, *Growing Slowly Wise.* As your interests and tastes mellow with age, your intensity modifies, and you really do desire the finer things of life—like true wisdom.

Smart has its place, but it comes with a personality. Smart has a competitive chip on his shoulder, making his case and drawing attention to himself. He often has a lot to offer, but needs a lot of polishing of his people skills.

If things get any worse, I'll have to ask you to stop
helping me.

Wise is the perfect lady or gentleman. Wise will sit waiting for an invitation, for the question, before interjecting themselves into a situation. While often being the experts, their humility quietly awaits the proper moment.

You must want wisdom so much that you will make room and adjust your world to let wisdom grow into your life. You can't go purchase two pounds of wisdom. Wisdom comes through experiencing life and learning in the process.

Knows Up! Wisdom can be learned both from others and from your own life experiences. You can go find it, or let it come to you. Just like your laptop goes searching for an internet connection, your desire for wisdom will prep you for many lessons.

Wisdom brings a dimension of life that will really bless you. Wisdom brings calm, peace, and awareness of a new level of reality that you will really be glad you have found. Keep pursuing wisdom! You will not be disappointed, but thrilled.

If you are not willing to learn, no one can help you.
If you are determined to learn, no one can stop you.

A wise old owl lived in an oak;
The more he saw, the less he spoke;
The less he spoke, the more he heard;
Why can't we all be like that wise old bird?

Discriminate

If you don't ask, the answer will always be "No."

Discriminate is a perfectly good word. It is a valuable tool the wise use effectively. It can benefit you just as much when you use it intelligently.

To discriminate means to make intelligent distinctions between things you are comparing. How else might you make wise decisions? Realistic information comparing two positions is crucial to achieving the best results.

Smart folks say discrimination "ain't fair!" You are picking on folks. You are not treating them equally.

The wise provide equal consideration and opportunity. The wise believe the best about others, and they can learn to self-talk themselves into a better future. They need to be empowered, not enabled!

Knows Up! You can empower folks who have the willing potential to advance. Become their mentor and cheerleader!

When in doubt, just take the next small step.

Believe

I AM an atheist. I swear to God I am!

A friend of mine said he was a believer. I asked him what he believed in. We both came to the conclusion he "believed in believing."

Believing can be a nebulous, unfocused something. My favorite bumper sticker reads *"Honk, if you believe in something or nothing, anything or everything!"* Is it reasonable to expect you must be able to define the "what and why" of what you believe?

Belief must have some object or person that defines your belief. It could be some guiding principle, or a religion, or a person. Belief in belief just won't cut it.

It would be best if you can describe the reasons for your beliefs. Your motivation and passion communicates your conviction that your belief system has value. In what ways do your beliefs benefit you and others?

Knows Up! Your belief system is yours for your own reasons and benefits. Live it out with passion and conviction.

Prayer: Don't give God instructions; just report for duty.

Sincerity

Ignore the bossy; listen to the encouragers.

Sincerity comes from the idea "without wax." Ancient pottery makers would take items with flaws or cracks, fill them with wax, and cover them over with paint. "Sincere" was an advertising word to indicate the authenticity of the product.

Sincerity today means honesty or genuineness. It very often describes behaviors. Unfortunately, while most frequently used as a positive modifier, it can also indicate the negative.

Eric Hofer wrote a short book, *The True Believer,* in the early 1950's. Sincerity was one of the foundational ideas. The deeper the belief, the greater the sincerity.

Could it be that some are sincerely wrong? Check out the levels of intensity on both sides of many belief systems. Can both sides be right, or wrong?

Knows Up! You can develop your belief system, moving from smart to wise. The more carefully you do, the better able you will be to communicate your understandings effectively.

An atheist's worst moment is being truly grateful with no one to thank.

Anchors

The way others treat people
says a lot about them—not you!

Is *anchor* a good word? I guess it depends on how you use it. Would you say, "hold down" or "drag down?"

It is good news when a boat anchor holds the boat in place. Buildings and bridges need to be firmly anchored. The wise are anchored with informed, trusted, principled ideas.

Anchor also can be used to "drag down." That could be somewhat destructive. But it might be good for the egomaniac to be dragged down to reality.

The wise see value in being anchored. Your life philosophy and operational values benefit when you are anchored in proven, substantive thought. Changing your mind like the weather changes is not being anchored.

Knows Up! The wisdom of the ages is available for your consideration. Choose wisely and become an anchored person.

A contented person is someone
who can enjoy the scenery along a detour.

Political Correctness

Give the devil an inch and he'll become a ruler.

Political correctness is the archenemy of wisdom. Political wisdom keeps gathering large numbers of converts. Might and numbers don't make political correctness right or wise.

Political correctness is energized by sophomoric enthusiasm. All of the squatters from the "Occupy America" crowd are enthusiastic supporters. Those who rob Peter to pay Paul will find many supporters for Paul!

"It ain't fair" and "it's not right!" Have you ever figured out how to make it fair, and make it right on a large, societal basis? It's all based on emotion rather than rational and reasonable solutions.

Wisdom encourages personal responsibility and using your life to benefit yourself and society. As President Kennedy said, "Ask not what your country can do for you; ask what you can do for your country!" "Political correctness" really is the takers living off the makers.

Knows Up! As you confront the "politically correct" crowd, don't let their destructive blather drag you down. Remain anchored to wisdom and aspire to inspire before you expire!

Democracy is four wolves and a lamb voting on what to have for lunch.

Wisdom

Judge a tree from its fruit, not from its leaves.

Wisdom is more than "skill at living." Wisdom is a personal operational system using time-proven principles and values to guide your life's behaviors. As you age, regular upgrades are needed.

Smart is a like a car without a driver. Smart is important. Knowledge and skill are the tools of living, but you need a wise and seasoned operator.

Think of the smart, tricky, sneaky, evil folks that have become "successful" at the destruction and abuse of others. These folks "love things and use (abuse) people!" The wise "use things and love people!"

Wisdom always takes the high road. Wisdom develops the substantive things that will last the ages, and contribute to developing lasting virtuous institutions. Wise people apply the "knows" to one and all, and celebrate the great positive progress of mankind.

Knows Up! Wisdom can be developed and grow in everyone. Determine to keep polishing your "knows" so they become effectively wise.

When you lose, don't lose the lesson.

 Coffee Break!

Laughter is an instant vacation.

Coffee in England always tastes
like a chemistry experiment.

> If I agreed with you,
> we'd both be wrong.

Don't criticize my coffee.
You may be old and weak one day.

> If you plan to fail, and then succeed,
> which have you done?

Is there life before coffee?
There is NO life before coffee.
There is life AFTER coffee!!

> Plan to be spontaneous tomorrow.

*Laughter is a tranquilizer with no side
effects.*

Is The Most Important Thing What You Do Next?

Does tomorrow ever arrive? The wise understand that reality limits life to today! You can't relive yesterday. Tomorrow never gets here. We live in units called today.

Expect the urgent to get in the way of the important Expect interruptions from anyone, or everyone. Life happens in a way you can't control. Keeping all your plates spinning at one time will prove challenging.

Reality is the leading cause of stress.

Blowing Your Knows In Public has been challenging you with many insights for you to consider. Your vision, coupled with an improved operating system, will provide you with the foundation for moving forward.

Hopefully, you are preparing your personal "Emancipation Proclamation." You are freeing yourself from all the unwanted, useless, troublesome rocks that have overloaded your backpack of life. You are thrilled by the freedom of traveling light with the growing gift of practical wisdom.

The ultimate reality is personal choice. You will be the "doer" of your future, building one day at a time. Looking back at your day-timer will show how you did spend your time, attention, and money each day.

Positive things happen to positive people.

The wise learn from their evaluation of preceding days and events. A simple "so far, so good" optimistic outlook can empower your continuation toward success.

But today brings today, which will end shortly. What is your agenda and action plan? Initiative is personal, activated by you. *Next* is your personal opportunity and responsibility.

Some things have to be believed to be seen.

You might be starting from scratch, or well on your way. The wise understand they must start anew every day. Being a self- starter to partner with your self-talk is an effective combination.

Your long-term action plan must be broken into smaller, manageable parts. Each day ends with reflection to determine your starting point the first thing on the following day.

It is easier to steer a moving car than a parked one.

Knows Up! Think of your success on the previous days. You continue to make daily investments and adjustments. Keep your eye on the prize and "get back at it!"

Your mental and emotional engagement will help you maintain a sense of momentum. You are continuing instead of starting over every day. Each day is one day further into your success.

Professor Perfection will show up on the job site at any time. He works 24/7/365. Anticipate his arrival at the worst possible times. Your instant response is, "Talk to the hand!"

You must be honest in your evaluation and keep empowering your self-talk. You will wander, waffle, and wonder. The wise get faster and faster in realizing their mental-emotional state and adjust rapidly, getting back on track and moving forward.

I let my mind wander, and it never came back.

Your personal, competitive excellence will be tested. You will have to battle your "won't power" with your "will power." Remember you control the gas pedal, brake, and steering in your vehicle of life. Keep your goal in mind.

All those great virtues of life motivate the wise. Courage, commitment, dedication, and intensity show up as the wise move forward. You really don't know if you have these wise virtues until you have to demonstrate them.

Nothing great was ever achieved without enthusiasm.
Emerson

Almost 20 years ago my father-in-law brought 20 "suitcase" trees from Michigan's Upper Peninsula to our Idaho mountain cabin. He dug up some very small balsam fir trees on the farm, washed off the dirt, packed them in wet newspaper, and brought them to Idaho in his suitcase. Today we have 20-foot trees that produce a beautiful Christmas tree smell when we rub the needles together. The tall dark green trees always remind us of the Gibbs City, Michigan homestead.

Rejoice that thorns have roses.

Your purposeful action will bring results that will bring joy to your life and bless all those around you. Every day you are planting those seeds that will produce a beneficial crop of accomplishments and memories.

Knows Up! Today is the day you have been waiting for. Make the "now" of every new day come alive enthusiastically to make a significant contribution to your enjoyable future.

So, what are you waiting for? "Next" has already arrived and awaits your creative efforts. Have a great today by making the good things happen. Enjoy today. It will be gone at midnight, just like Cinderella's story.

One of these days is none of these days.

Prioritize

Yesterday was the deadline for all complaints. Sorry!

Have you ever put your pants on and then your underwear? How well do your socks fit over your shoes? So, does it matter—the order in which we do things?

The more complicated the project or process, the more critical prioritizing our actions becomes. There is a serious difference between activity and productivity. Wisdom makes prioritizing an operational mandate.

Did you ever shoot your mouth off, realize what you just said, and then tried to reach out and grab your words before they reached someone's ear? Sounds kind of funny, but I bet you have thought or done just that. *"Please put your brain in gear before you put your mouth in motion."*

Proactive people are "get-it-done" kind of folks. You want to be a positive influence on life. It is your nature to get after things.

Knows Up! Reflective, prioritized thinking and actions are a learned skill and process. Pursuing that type of wisdom is a noble pursuit.

Your children get only one childhood.

Action

Give me ambiguity or give me something else.

"Lights, Camera, Action" appears a lot in movies and cartoons. I'm not sure if that is really how it happens, but it contains a wise understanding. After all the practice and preparation, there comes a time for action!

As a former track starter, what if I only told the runners, "Ready, Set?" What if there wasn't a starter on your car? There is a time for action: *Now!*

Wisdom knows the place of action. Action must take place in the proper place and sequence. "Fire, Ready, Aim" won't cut it.

Wisdom also realizes that every morning presents a new challenge. Your self-talk is preparation for positive, purposeful action. Just "saying so don't make it so!"

Knows Up! You are totally capable and encouraged to do the next *"Now!"* Keep taking those positive action steps toward a better future.

No matter how you feel, get up, dress up, and show up!

Timing

If you can't run with the big dogs,
stay on the porch.

Traveling with the 1964 North Park College summer quartette, I learned an unforgettable lesson in timing. We were singing an old Negro spiritual in San Jose, California. At a certain point, I was supposed to join in.

Tim did his part, and I totally spaced it. Suddenly, the other three guys gave me "the look!" Tim nodded, started over, and the song ended successfully.

Timing is important in both the world of smart and wise. Plans and expectations are built on timing and integration of all the parts. *"Next"* demands that good timing is understood, mastered and done—on time.

The smart approach timing as a "have to." The wise see timing as a "want to." Proper timing is the noble and best way to accomplish things that are important.

Knows Up! While your rhythm might leave much to be desired, you can master being on time. The wise respect and give the gift of showing up "on time."

You will always find it
in the last place you look.

Strategy

If you don't step forward, you will always be in the same place.

"Gramp's Camp" is when the grandkids come to the mountains without their parents. Part of the time we have "work" parties. Many kids today don't have the chance to learn how to work.

Whether it was building the deck or loading logs into the trailer, my strategy was to make the kids think. I told them what I wanted done, and asked them what to do next. Very often it became a class in applied physics.

Doing anything without some idea of strategy seems futile. Building anything implies putting it together. Moving from the parts to successful completion demands a *"doing"* strategy.

My problem with evolution involves strategy. How did "nothing" become the incredibly complicated universe where we now live? Did it really happen by chance?

Knows Up! You can learn to become strategic. Your wisdom will skyrocket as you learn strategy.

You have to crack a few eggs to make an omelet.

Paradigm

Over-prepare, then go with the flow.

Now, *paradigm* sounds like a word dripping with wisdom. If you can't dazzle them with brilliance, baffle them with balderdash. Smart likes to show off, but wisdom wants to educate.

A paradigm is a statement describing a pattern of thinking. Paradigms take information, values, and actions, and tell others what you think, believe, and understand. Wisdom demonstrates a well-organized mind.

Many one-liners could be your paradigm. It is a small package of words communicating something practical, wise, or true. Like a mini-skirt it must be short enough to be interesting, but long enough to cover the subject.

Wisdom organizes thoughts into statements communicating a message. The message shares wisdom in words folks can easily understand. Wisdom that blows over the heads of readers or past the ears of your listeners is wasted.

Knows Up! You can learn to organize your thoughts into wise paradigms. Both you and your listeners will be encouraged and educated by the organization of your wisdom.

It's nice to be important,
but it's more important to be nice.

Self-Talk

The biggest obstacle is between our ears.

They say many statistics are made up on the spot. I once heard that the average man talks with other people about 30 minutes a day. That must mean he spends the rest of the time talking to himself!

Whatever the actual numbers, we do spend most of our time talking to ourselves. We talk ourselves into and out of things, encourage or criticize, build up, or break down. The wise reflect and analyze those internal conversations.

I used to think choice is the ultimate reality. Self-talk is the biggest choice we constantly make. Almost everything we do is empowered by our self-talk.

Blowing Your Knows In Public concludes that just about everything we have considered is connected to our self-talk. We do constantly tell ourselves what to do, say, and think. Adding a large dose of wisdom would be highly beneficial.

Knows Up! You are very smart and skilled at talking to yourself. The next step to effective maturity is using the filter of wisdom with your self-talk.

The key to failure is trying to please everyone.
Bill Cosby

Coffee Break!

Laughter is an instant vacation.

Deja Brew:
The feeling that you've had this coffee before.

Did you ever see the headline,
"Psychic Wins Lottery?"

I make serious coffee so strong
it wakes up the neighbors!!!

What's another word for thesaurus?

Stealing someone's coffee is called "mugging."

How much faith does it take to be an atheist?

Laughter is a tranquilizer with no side effects.

Let's Keep On Moving From Smart To Wise

Keep gathering the new and improved "smarts" that will empower your next season of life. Celebrate the wise lessons that are becoming your traveling partners throughout your life.

Both of these concepts demand action. They are something you must do. They are not produced instantly, but are part of the processes of life. Just like your age keeps moving on, so must your wisdom development keep moving onward and upward.

"Well done is better than well said." Benjamin Franklin

The benefits of wisdom always exceed the cost. You will rejoice at the truths of wise living. The costs of avoiding wisdom will become very telling.

Knows Up! ***When the going gets tough, the tough get tougher.*** Now figure out a similar one-liner about wisdom. While it's good to "toughen up" for the journey, it's far greater still to "wise up!" Wisdom is within your grasp. Go for it!

Lead, follow, or get out of the way! It's your life!

*During the last several years of teaching, I kept posting one-liners on bright neon paper around my classroom. I settled on two signs right behind my desk: **"Quit doing stupid stuff,"** and **"What part of NO don't you understand?"***

Moving from smart to wise might be summed up in those too short thoughts. The wise are constantly working to do things right the first time. The wise have also learned that knowing often comes from aggressive pursuit of those wise lessons worth experiencing.

Knows Up! You might get spooked that wisdom is like eating the whole smorgasbord in one sitting. Nothing can be further from the truth. Wisdom comes in bite-size portions. Wisdom can be learned with your direct attention.

Separate the "fact" from the "fluff."
Don't settle for the sizzle.

Expect that the world of multi-media will provide constant drumming of images, thoughts, and advertising, seeking your acceptance. You had best prep and remind yourself that this barrage will be continuous and endless. You must master the use of filters and "ear plugs" to survive. Your goals have a significantly higher value and purpose. Battle on!

My personal counsel is to "respect the process!" There are many motivating models, like a plant growing. Have you ever seen a piece of fruit hanging on a tree agonizing, grunting, and fretting in order to grow? Wisdom is best developed through calm introspection and reflection.

Watch out! Some of my best mistakes have not yet been made!

Keep a sharp eye out for Professor Perfection. *If you aren't willing to make mistakes, don't expect to make anything.* In baseball the best hitters only get three or four hits out of ten times at bat!

Knows Up! Mistakes and failures are often the classroom where wisdom is taught. Fear of failure often paralyzes us. Remember, some of the greatest discoveries came through the lessons learned and applied in failure.

Some folks are driven to succeed. They have aggressive plans to make lots of money, become famous, or are always working hard to improve their resumé. The acquisition of wisdom occurs often in a passive and calm manner. Wisdom often sneaks up beside you and whispers, *"Did you catch that?"* or *"See what I have been telling you?"* Often you might see it in your rearview mirror.

Pride brings inverse results: our head swells and our mind shrinks.

Wisdom is never arrogant or overbearing. Wisdom is not compelled to "blow its knows." Wisdom is not an accumulation to be shown off and paraded. Wisdom shows up calmly and effectively while living daily a beneficial and purposeful life. Wisdom is not a prize to be grabbed, but a lifestyle to be lived which benefits the owner and all he is connected to in life.

The wise are always taking the position of a student. Knowing always comes from learning. The greatest lessons help one on to a better, more enjoyable, and rewarding lifestyle. The wise do not resist, rebuff, or complain about learning since they have a long history of beneficial lessons.

It is a rare person who wants to hear
what he doesn't want to hear.

Remember the Dr. Seuss's quote to start this book: *"No one is Youer than you!"* Believe that you really are an incredible, unique package. Also believe the amazing benefits of continuing to master the gift of wisdom.

The secret of wisdom is as unique as you. You have to welcome wisdom into your life. "Respect the process!" Wisdom will meet you frequently and unexpectedly. Keep your ears, eyes, mind and emotions anticipating its arrival. You won't be disappointed. Just keep being "FAT"—faithful, available and teachable.

Knows Up! Keep living life in daily packages. Be your own best friend, counselor, and cheerleader. Keep your cool. Take frequent five-minute vacations while wisdom quietly takes residence in your life.

The only place where success comes before work
is in the dictionary!

Who?

*A man's character is like a fence—
all the whitewash in the world
won't strengthen it.*

Who me? Yes, you! Wisdom depends on you!

Wisdom from a book, teacher, or library only has potential; the goal of wisdom is becoming alive and empowering your life. There is virtually no use for wisdom until it produces benefits in your life. Wisdom only has real value when changing your life.

Wisdom is no "phony-baloney" cheap charlatan. Wisdom is the authentic, guaranteed real deal. The wisdom of the ages is a time-proven product.

The Bible contains generation upon generation of folks who have come to understand, live, and prove the truths of wise living. You, too, can become a part of that long line of successful, life- changing wisdom and good news.

Knows Up! It is not so mysterious and improbable. Jesus invites you personally to follow along as He teaches, encourages, and wonderfully changes *your* life.

**You have to make it through the day
to enjoy the sunset.**

What?

I have had amnesia as long as I can remember.

"Lights on, anybody home?" is a fun line checking to see if you are awake and paying attention. Wisdom is best enhanced when you are wide-awake, sharp, and on top of your game. Since wisdom brings such fantastic benefits, it is best to give it your best shot.

So, what, really, is wisdom? Since we are so busy talking about it, what is wisdom? Wisdom sounds somewhat overpowering, hard to comprehend and fully grasp.

The best teachers are able to explain things like the fruit being on the lowest branches so everyone can grasp ahold of it. Wisdom is like that—explain it first for beginners. Wisdom contains the seed with an automatic growth hormone already contained.

Wisdom is processed learning transformed into beneficial living skills. It is the type of learning that empowers, improves and is an all around "pick-me-up" for life. It really does make life better.

Knows Up! Wisdom is user-friendly. Somehow wisdom senses your needed lesson, and provides it clearly, effectively and productively.

Worry is a squatter; it must be evicted!

When?

Do you need another day between Saturday and Sunday?

"Are we there yet, Daddy?" As a kid, you didn't understand the traveling process. The anticipation and start were real, but the "when" seemed to take forever.

"When" is always important in a news story. "When" puts events in proper sequence, time, and place. As Jack Webb in the 1950's TV show "Dragnet" always said, "The facts ma'am, just the facts!"

Wisdom has a past and a future. For your consideration and benefit, "when" is now. You can both desire and enjoy the growing benefits both now and on into the future.

Wisdom is not static; it needs your active involvement. Gathering input, contemplating it in reference to your life, and activating it by using it in your life, produces the "when" of benefit. You need to keep cranking it up and ramrodding the process.

Knows Up! Wisdom is not some "pie in the sky by and by." Wisdom begins when you start up the process. **If not now, when? If not you, who?**

Everyday is a gift; that's why they call it the present.

Where?

Some folks would rather look at the map than actually visit the place.

From the perspective of wisdom, you are the "where!" Your desire is that wisdom empowers your life right where you are, right now. You are ready, willing, and able. Bring it on!

"You will always find it in the last place you look!" You have been searching and looking for wisdom. Now that you are starting to find it, you need a place to put it!

In your situation, you must keep two thoughts always in mind: place and action. Wisdom needs a parking place where it is immediately available for use. Instant retrieval and implementation demonstrate wise preparation.

The task is not completed; it never ends. You are constantly upgrading and improving. Just like the invitation of Jesus: keep following, learning, and mastering the lessons from the Master Teacher.

Knows Up! Your experience in wise living will start now and grow exponentially. Getting the best input from the Master will produce unbelievable growth and benefits with wise and effective living.

If you come to a fork in the road, TAKE IT!

How?

A verbal contract is not worth the paper it is written on.

"How?" has a built-in secret. The question demands an answer. "How" indicates an insight to successful completion of a task.

My grandsons are such fun to watch grow up. When they get a new gift or project, their "how gene" automatically takes over. They will figure out the "how." Stand aside!

"How" is a strong indicator of your desire. When asking "how," you are actively seeking input for solutions. You sense and understand your need, and desire to keep moving forward on your quest.

Empower the motivation of your "how." Use your curiosity to energize your search and application. You and others will benefit from the wisdom gathered and implemented.

Knows Up! Plenty of accomplished solutions and wisdom are readily awaiting your finding and retrieval. Maybe you will be the one to answer "how" to the major, unanswered questions of today.

Age doesn't always bring wisdom; sometimes, it comes alone.

Why?

You can't have everything...
where would you put it?

The undocumented story tells of a philosophy professor who had a one-word question on his final exam. "Why?" Most students were bamboozled and terrified.

With his final grade resting on his answer, the student answered, "Why not!" Much to the other students' amazement and confusion to such an immediate answer, he turned in his paper and left. The story goes that he did get his "A" in the class.

Why ask "why?" It really is up to you! You do things to answer your own questions in life, for your own reasons.

Your motivation and quest is what makes it yours. Enjoy the freedom of your choices and journey. You really are uniquely you.

Knows Up! Your "why" does not need the approval of others. It is your choice, so choose wisely, and empower your choices with determined self-talk!

Dream, then Do!

Coffee Break!

Laughter is an instant vacation.

*Forever: Time it takes to brew the
first pot of coffee in the morning.*

Can atheists get insurance for acts of God?

*I bought a decaffeinated coffee table;
you can't even see the difference.*

How do a fool and his money GET together?

*Don't drink coffee in the morning.
It will keep you awake until noon.*

**A fine is a tax for doing wrong.
A tax is a fine for doing well.**

*Laughter is a tranquilizer with no side
effects.*

Listen to Him.
So, Who's "Him?"

What place does listening play in the transitioning from smart to wise? How do you come up with the right questions? Even with the best questions, where do you look to start to find the answers?

Every speaker or writer is advocating some message. It must be important to them. The wise always listen for the best a speaker has to offer! It is mandatory for the wise to understand the best that is being suggested.

"Saying so don't make it so!"

While the speaker is emphasizing what is best from his viewpoint, the wise are always asking, is that message the best for me, and for mankind? The wise have developed ways to separate the substance from the sizzle, truth from fiction, wise from smart.

While it might make perfect sense, and be enthusiastically delivered, every message will be filtered by the wise. The wise do not get caught up in the passion and power of the delivery; they calmly define and evaluate the best the message has to offer.

> *The workshop began right on time. The speaker was properly introduced and began his talk. My curiosity was constantly wandering over to a stool with an old rotary phone sitting on top. What's the deal with that phone? The first session ended. About ten minutes into the second session the phone began ringing. The speaker ignored the ringing and continued speaking. After what seemed to be an extra long time of the phone ringing, someone in the back finally shouted,* **"Answer the @#&% phone!"**

The speaker had the last laugh. After challenging us to share our discomfort and distraction about the ringing phone, he used that experience to challenge the audience about what lessons can be learned, remembered, and applied to our lives.

Why do you answer the phone? You really don't have to. Just let it ring. Why do you have caller ID, or an answering machine? The reality is that everyone is curious about "who" is calling, and "what" might be the content of the call. If we expect or anticipate a positive message, we will readily answer the call.

What do you want to hear?

The wise have developed and mastered a sincere desire to be asking the right questions, at the right time, in the right way, of the right people. The wise proactively seek out wherever the path of truth may lead them. Being in constant dialogue, their never-ending openness to the best moves them forward in their quest for wisdom.

The wise understand that many of the most passionate voices reside on a one-way street where U-turns are not permitted. The wise know it is a lot easier to stay out of trouble than to get out of trouble. Caution is always the best policy in major considerations.

When they want your opinion, they will give it to you!

So what are the wise really pursuing? Wisdom desires a total operational paradigm where the best in every field of understanding comes together to maximize life and interactions with the world and fellow mankind.

Looking for love in all the wrong places.
Waylon Jennings

Like the country western song suggests, the wise go looking. Just like the prospectors of old, you never know where you might find the mother lode, and strike it rich. Those prospectors followed the best information available, but had to get out into the wild and start digging.

Reality will definitely inform you when you are looking in the right places or wrong places. My hometown of Stambaugh, Michigan became a reality when Harvey Mellon was exploring and was wise enough to recognize the red rock in an outcropping of a side hill was iron ore.

Many a prospector became very excited with their discoveries until the assessor came back with the report— *fool's gold.* The wise are open to the process, and journey to wisdom, not "phony-baloney, feel-good, rock and roll."

There is a significant difference between a good, sound reason, and a reason that sounds good!

Living in the Idaho Mountains where the next small communities are at least 45 minutes away, our volunteer fire district and ambulance group provide a very important service to our community. We must come together to help each other out. When the phone rings, or radio tone-out comes, volunteers have committed to drop everything and respond. We never know what to expect, but we show up to help as best we can.

The wise are responders! They process the events and ideas that life brings them. Being open, aware, and curious, they are always interested in the new stuff coming down the pike. The wise understand some of the new stuff might prove highly beneficial.

The unofficial motto of the Coast Guard goes something like "You don't have to come back; you have to GO!" The Coast Guard has responded in the worst of conditions to rescue those in trouble. They commit to responding regardless of the reality presented.

If you do not go after what you want, you will never get it.

Resisters have their own reasons for hanging back and dragging their feet. Whether it be that their life is too complicated, confusing, or challenging, they resist being open to new possibilities. They choose to stay stuck inside their struggling comfort zone; their plates are already too full.

One of the major issues of life is the concept of God. Responders embrace the quest for understanding; whereas, the resisters often respond with disinterest.

If God really does exist, it really does matter in the great scheme of things. One could seriously benefit from finding out where the truth of the matter might exist. The wise pursue; the resisters move on to other things.

Theology is the study of god/gods. "Ology" means study, and "theos" means god or gods. It is important to understand that theology is man's attempt to make sense out of the question of God. Where do theologians get their raw material to start building a theology of god?

Man's way leads to a hopeless end;
God's way leads to endless hope.

Religion is man's organizational attempt to bring together people of common understandings about God. Since they believe the same things, they come together to live out their guiding principles. Most often they have rational intentions and good will.

Someone has said religion was invented by man, for man, to control man. It is very informative to observe all the different religions of the world. The incredible diversity of religion leads to tremendous confusion. How can there be any consensus when the world's religions demonstrate very few areas of agreement?

***Honk if you believe in something, or nothing,
in anything, or everything.***

Among all the religious personalities there is one called Jesus Christ. Is Jesus just another religious leader among the many seeking your allegiance? Is he just like everyone else, and you lump them all together, and then resist and reject the whole bunch?

Do you find it interesting that those voices with a negative viewpoint of God and Jesus Christ have nothing good or positive to offer instead of Jesus? What really are their best insights and solutions? Do they have a positive alternative, or their *good news?*

Where do you turn to find out the best information about a subject? Would you ask a Chicago Bear's fan about their hated rival, the Green Bay Packers? Would you ask a life long Democrat about the truth of the Republican Party? It is always best to go to the original source, pursue truth, and find out for yourself.

***It is unbelievable what unbelievable things
an unbeliever will believe
in order to be an unbeliever.***

A common trait of all religions is that mankind is trying to "get to God." Often the goal of religious behaviors and understandings is to influence and impress God, so that God will grant acceptance and provide favor, so man can live in the "heavenly hereafter."

At funerals, the comment is often heard that the loved one has moved on to a better place. Are those statements based on hard, factual evidence or some mental-emotional creation to ease the pain of a loved one passing?

Urgent matters are seldom important;
important matters are seldom urgent!

The wise ask the tough questions, wade through thorough investigation, pursuing wise answers and understanding. How, really, is eternity determined? Where does one really spend eternity? Who makes the final judgments?

Jesus did not come to start a religion. Jesus did not come to endorse any religion or denomination. Jesus became man to show, tell, and communicate God's message of love, forgiveness, redemption, and salvation.

Jesus is the One Person who can change your life.

God does not have any grandchildren. The Bible makes it very clear that it is an individual relationship, first generation only. You can't ride on anyone's coattails. Jesus Christ desires a personal friend, a relationship with *you!*

Jesus can't see a crowd or group. He only sees individuals one at a time. His invitation is personal—*given directly to you.* You have the tremendous opportunity to accept and start your journey towards Him. He most likely is already walking with you.

Incline your ear, and come to me;
hear, that your soul may live! Isaiah 55: 3 (**ESV**)

It is valuable to point out that some voices have long and established critical opinions about Jesus Christ. As a sincere seeker of the truth about Jesus Christ, it would be best to consider the source of the best about Jesus. Your considerations have eternal consequences.

When an agnostic dies, does he go to the "great perhaps?"

There is a reason that the Bible is the greatest selling book of all history. The Bible tells the long story of God's involvement with peoples from the beginning of time. The Old Testament points to Jesus coming. The New Testament tells the story of Jesus's birth, life, death, and resurrection. It's an amazing true story.

The opening thought of this section is that the wise figure out what the best any spokesman has to offer. In the Christmas story, the arrival of Jesus Christ was first announced to some lowly shepherds. The angel startled the shepherds who were out watching their flocks in the dark of night.

> *"Don't be afraid," he said. "I bring you the most joyful news ever announced, and it is for everyone! The Savior—yes, the Messiah, the Lord—has been born tonight in Bethlehem!"*
> Luke 2:10-11 [Life Application Bible. The Living New Testament]

Have you ever heard a speaker or writer make such a universal statement of the *best?* The Christian message is called the "Gospel –Good News!" If this really is the universal *best* message ever announced, would you be wise enough to seriously investigate?

The wise have proper respect for earned credentials. Wisdom knows where to look and who gets heard. Consider how the Gospel of Mark validates Jesus Christ:

> **"And a voice came out of the heavens, Thou art my beloved Son, in thee I am well pleased."** Mark 1:11 [ESV]

God Himself validates and recognizes Jesus as his Son. The first chapter of John's gospel tells how Jesus became a man, and became a living part of the human experience. Someone coined the phrase that aptly describes this amazing event, "God in a Bod!" Jesus became the greatest living audio-visual in history.

One of the names given to Jesus is Immanuel, meaning, "God is with us." God is not some distant, philosophical construct from the mind of mankind. God is a living participant in the life of the world, residing in the person of Jesus Christ, empowered by His Holy Spirit, no matter what the critics may say.

The Big Bang theory: God spoke, and "Bang"—it happened!

God believes He is rather self evident, unconcerned whether you can prove His existence or not. It is very informative to consider those folks who work so long and hard to prove beyond a doubt that God does not exist.

Everyone throughout his or her life works to construct his life equation for a successful, enjoyable life. In a mathematical equation, every factor must be processed to get the correct answer. Some folks purposefully choose to omit the God/Jesus factor from their life equation. Problem solved. Or is it?

> *"This continues to be the Gospel of Welcome, and the only one who wouldn't be welcome is the one who doesn't want to be—someone who thinks, for one reason or another, that they do not need it."*
>
> The Catch, John Fischer

The wise learn to know who to listen to, and where to turn for the best information. What they say to themselves after careful research is more valued than the conclusions others may have reached.

Life always offers you a second chance; it is called tomorrow!

Jesus on His own was, and continues to be, one of the most consequential personalities of all history. Reflect on the following comments about Jesus Christ. Might Jesus be worth your consideration?

> *Nineteen centuries have come and gone, and today Jesus is the central figure of the human race, and the leader of mankind's progress. All the armies that have ever marched, all the navies that have ever sailed, all the parliaments that have ever sat, all the kings that ever reigned put together have not affected the life of mankind on earth as powerfully as **that one solitary life**.*   Dr. James Allan © 1926.

Many who become interested in Jesus Christ need to know Jesus has already begun the connection process. Through His very powerful Holy Spirit, He continues to send the invitation to every interested person: "Follow Me, and I will…" [Mark 1:17 ESV]

"Jesus used many such illustrations to teach the people as much as they were ready to understand."
Mark 4:33 [NLT]

As you seek to learn more about Jesus, His Holy Spirit will empower your seeking, and give understanding. For centuries, mankind has read the Bible with the life changing good news. God's Holy Spirit is always actively pointing individuals towards Jesus Christ. You, included!

Your willingness and desire to learn and find out about Jesus is the major factor in beginning your understanding of Jesus. He is already active behind the scenes. Gut check time. Will you Respond or Resist?

A will is a dead giveaway.

Remember Waylon Jennings's song, "Looking For Love In All The Wrong Places?" It really does matter where we go looking for love, truth, or anything important. It also sounds like we are totally responsible for the looking process. But consider the Christian position.

Whether Waylon knew it or not, further on in his song he states a very powerful Christian message:

*"You came a-knocking at my heart's door.
You're everything I've been looking for."*

John Stott wrote *Why I am a Christian.* In his first chapter, "The Hound of Heaven," John credits Jesus Christ and His Holy Spirit for being the major factor in his becoming a Christian follower of Jesus. Jesus kept coming after him.

John validates Waylon's country western theology. Jesus, The Hound of Heaven, really does "come a-knocking at my heart's door." Millions over the centuries, in countries all around the world have experienced, "You're everything I've been looking for."

What do I need to hear that I don't want to hear?

"Ponder anew what the Almighty can do," is a phrase in a song we sang at church last week. Consider it a personal invitation and challenge. God is not some Johnny-come-lately, the new kid on the block. The greatest evidence is the billions of changed lives over the centuries.

You are invited! Most of the invitations of Jesus in the Bible are followed with Jesus saying something like, *"I will..."* Following Jesus is not some "fourth quarter, suck it up, and let's win one for the Gipper!" choice. Through the indwelling power of His Holy Spirit, and the gift of prayer, Jesus is your constant traveling companion, host, and professor. Jesus will give you a new heart and head, a new way of thinking and feeling, motivating you to love and encourage yourself and others. Rejoice—you really are loved and forgiven. Accept the gift joyfully.

In the process of learning and following Jesus, you are offered the most important gift, the forgiveness of your sin. Sin leads you to an eternal separation from God.

God gives you the free choice of where you desire to spend eternity. Jesus died for your sins so you can spend eternity in God's Heaven. Ask for forgiveness and accept the gift of eternal salvation gladly.

Without Christ—a hopeless end.
With Christ—endless hope!

My little four-step process might help you understand the process of following Jesus:

1. *"I got to!"* You start to realize you are the one who needs to start the journey towards being a willing and teachable student about Jesus.

2. *"I get to!"* Your head and heart start to realize this is an informative and exciting world that is not a bunch of rules, but a lifestyle where you get to enjoy all the benefits of belonging to the family of God!

3. *"I want to!"* The process keeps empowering you until you really want to learn, understand, and grow. Your excitement keeps you pursuing wisdom and truth.

4. *"I love to!"* When you love to do something, you don't have to be reminded, and you don't have to work at it. You just love it and live it, almost automatically.

I can only give you my most enthusiastic endorsement. As one of our Young Life kids used to say in the '80's, *"Hey man, what the fat: Jesus Christ is where it's at!"*

You are encouraged to find a friend who loves and follows Jesus Christ. Ask them to tell you about Jesus Christ. Do not ask them about religion or church. Your focus is learning to love and follow Jesus. Find a friend to journey with you.

To help you get started, let me recommend some reading:

1. Acquire an easy to read *Life Application Bible*, then focus your first year on reading and re-reading Matthew, Mark, Luke, and John. These four gospels tell the story of Jesus by four men who personally knew, lived with, and followed Jesus.

2. Get a copy of *The Way of the Wise*, by Dr. Kevin Leman. Kevin is a college friend who is a psychologist, professor, and humorist. His book is full of wisdom and insight about Jesus.

3. Read *Who Is This Man?* by John Ortberg. John is a pastor and author who is very easy to read, full of wisdom and insight. This book is the most powerful introduction to Jesus I've read.

4. Another treasure is *Why I Am A Christian* by John Stott. John is one of the most trusted and revered Christian apologists. He is deeply respected for his wisdom, truth, and insight.

Let me end *Blowing Your Knows In Public* with the words John Stott uses as he ends his book. Jesus, John, and I invite you to take this first step, begin, and then continue following Jesus, just how every follower of Jesus started.

"I wonder if you, my reader, are ready to take the same step? If so, perhaps you would find it helpful to get away

and alone somewhere, and to echo this prayer, making it
your own:

A Prayer:

Lord Jesus Christ,
> *I am aware that in different ways you have been*
> *seeking me.*
> *I have heard you knocking at my door.*
> *I believe---*
>> *that your claims are true;*
>> *that you died on the cross for my sins,*
>> *and that you have risen in triumph over*
>> *death.*
> *Thank you for your loving offer of forgiveness,*
>> *freedom, and fulfillment.*

Now---
>> *I turn from my sinful self-centeredness.*
>> *I come to you as my Savior.*
>> *I submit to you as my Lord.*
> *Give me strength to follow you for the rest of my*
> *life.   Amen."*

The only question is Jesus Christ.
The only answer is Jesus Christ.

Reality

Reality defines itself!

Are you really living? Are you ready to die? Reality is made up of these two words.

In some ways there is no way to finesse reality. In the simplest terms, we live and then we die. Are there any other options?

Where do you get your ideas on what it really means to be fully alive? You are constantly bombarded with countless messages and propaganda. You determine your reality by those you listen to and how you respond.

Listening is "wanting to hear." Wisdom is listening to the best and truest voices. True wisdom is living out those best messages.

Knows Up! You personally have the opportunity and freedom to choose your best. You are always preparing for both now and eternity. Don't get snookered!

**Treat each day as your last;
one day you will be right.**

Know Your Place!

Sleep tight; God is up and on duty all night.

Do you remember being "put in your place?" Your parents and teachers ordered you where to go and what to do. As you continue to pursue wisdom, you can find your place and greatly improve your "skill at living."

Feeling like you are someplace else, and uncertain as to where you really should be, is understandable and confusing. Wise folks have processed life and determined their best fit. This is where I choose to fit in, and I'm working hard on what to do.

Expect plenty of suggestions coming at you from every direction. The wise have sorted out the voices and are always moving in their best directions. Your two biggest choices in life are whom you listen to, and how you control your self-talk.

God does speak through the Bible. Several times He tell us to listen to Jesus! Is there really a more important and authoritative voice worth hearing and understanding?

Knows Up! You can choose to listen to any voice. The wise make the best choices. Certainly, Jesus is a true source so you really can know the best wisdom for now and eternity.

The Bible is meant to be bread for daily use, not to be cake for special occasions.

Curious

The best time to start thinking about your retirement is before the boss does.

Why did "curiosity kill the cat?" On a scale of 1-10, how curious are you? What are you itching to know?

Look at the internet, magazines, and newspapers and you will see a tremendous curiosity about gossip, celebrities, and trivia. Who determines what really is important? The wise know they control their search and investigation for truth, and how their self- talk finalizes their answers.

Your curiosity, or lack of snooping and sniffing out important stuff, will determine where you end up in life. Wisdom understands the benefit of choosing wisely. Knowing the best and wisest will determine where you end up in this life and the next.

There is a huge world of ideas and interests out there. You are free to snoop, sniff, and settle in countless places. The wise make the best of their curiosity.

Knows Up! It's your life and future. "Carpe diem: seize the day!" The quality of your life, both here and forever, rests on your choices and self-talk.

Are you more interested in God changing your situation, or your heart and mind?

Download!

Success is not a thing to be waited for, it is a thing to be achieved.

Your computer only "knows" and can use only what is loaded or downloaded. Your computer can't create stuff on its own. It's the same with you. You are responsible to learn so that you can know!

Here's hoping you have *not* learned about all the bad stuff you can download in life. *Learn from the experiences of others; don't be the other!* You don't have to personally experience all the bad stuff life has to offer.

The Bible encourages us to "Rejoice and be exceedingly glad." So where can we download that type of insight and good news? I'm all for gladness and joy. Download now!

The wise are very selective in their downloads. They know they are choosing between good news and bad news. You really are downloading your future for now and for eternity.

Knows Up! You can download all the important wisdom by careful searching. Make sure to download the life-changing story of Jesus. Then listen to Him!

The more I want to get it done, the less I call it work.

Digest

Success isn't the result of spontaneous combustion; you must set yourself on fire...

Digest. Now, that is a life building, interesting word. Digestion is the process where the nutrition in food becomes you. Can you process the truth and insights of wisdom so that they become you?

Is there such a word as "wisdoming?" Maybe we can coin a new word describing how wisdom becomes an operational part of our "knows." "Wisdoming" becomes the wise empowering of our "knows."

Since wisdom is skill at living, having a certain measure of wisdom just adds to our collection. Putting your supper on your arm would sure look foolish. Wisdom is empowered action at living.

Smart just collects stuff, where wisdom uses stuff for purposeful living. It is easy to live out the best of wisdom, because it produces such fantastic results.

Knows Up! God gave us the Holy Spirit to help us with our wisdoming. Just keep reading the story of Jesus, and the Holy Spirit will keep bringing to life the wisdom from God Himself!

Some people dream of success, while others wake up and work hard on it.

Activate!
Your future always depends on what you are doing now!

Do you remember the frustration coming from your parents saying, "Batteries not included?" Little children are ready to explode with excitement and anticipation from their unbelievable, fantastic fantabulous new gift. They cannot comprehend why the present won't work.

Their exuberant excitement is only exceeded by their enormous disappointment. Wisdom has learned the lesson of activation. There comes a time when all the details are finally coming together, and now is the time for activation.

Standing at the starting line for a race, standing on the top of a ski run, or sitting down to a fancy restaurant meal is useless if you don't activate. Until you accept the invitation from Jesus to "come and see," nothing will change. Begin the process of following Jesus, and you will not be disappointed.

Every medicine contains an active ingredient that makes the medicine effective. The story and message of Jesus is empowered by the Holy Spirit of God. A serious desire to follow on your part will be met with a serious empowering of your coming to understand the truth and eternal wisdom of Jesus.

Knows Up, my friend! Jesus is The Way, The Truth, and The Life! He will activate your success in this life and the next.

The road to success has many tempting parking places.

Come!

The Spirit of God uses the Word of God to change hearts, minds, and lives.

RSVP requests a response on your part. If someone was kind enough to invite you, courtesy demands your acceptance or rejection. *If you were invited by a psychic, would you have to respond?*

"Come" is an invitation, not a command. Jesus uses "come" to indicate he doesn't demand you agree. He desires that you respond positively and come to find out what he is has in mind for you.

It is always a wise move to consider the source of the invitation. Jesus has the credentials like no one ever. He simply states that he really is God in a Bod!

"GOD" on His business card would be a huge understatement. If Jesus really is God, as millions upon millions believe, would you benefit from checking Him out? If true, the consequences are more than huge.

Knows Up! Jesus is knowable, understandable, and the real source of eternal wisdom. His gift to you is a new head, new heart, and new life.

Don't give up. Moses was once a basket case.

Follow!

God will give you direction,
but you have to do the walking.

As kids, we loved to play "Follow The Leader." The game was fun because I had several friends that were courageous and creative. Later—on our bikes, or while skiing—it often turned into a challenging adventure.

The leader made the game. They could make it so easy that is was no fun. The opposite was true if nobody could do what the leader proposed for us.

"If you are leading and no one is following, you are just going for a walk." Leading implies and expects followers. A one-person demonstration parade falls flat on its face.

The story of Jesus is like no other story in all of history. A baby born in a stable changes the course of history. *Many believe history really is His-story!*

Knows Up! Following Jesus has a fantastic upside. You are dearly loved by this leader. Find out why he gave His life so you can live a new life, both for now and eternity.

We don't change God's message;
His message changes us.

Me

As God becomes bigger in your life, problems become smaller.

What do you think and feel about "I-me-my" folks? At first, they are always talking about themselves. Then it turns to *"If I want your opinion, I'll give it to you!"*

Some leaders are full of themselves, always telling you what to do, what to think, and what to say. They make you feel privileged to be in their presence. The wise always respond with extreme caution.

Wisdom reminds you of *your* free choice in responding to any leader. Since you will receive or endure the consequences, be very selective with your following.

I like the title of the book, *Evidence That Demands A Verdict*, by Josh McDowell. Can any leader convince you of their authority, responsibility, and competence? Wisdom also demands a verdict when choosing to follow any leader.

Knows Up! The proof is in the pudding! Jesus has, and continues to bring, the incredible life changing *Good News* to billions of followers in the past, the present, and for eternity.

When you can't put it into words, God already understands.

Rejoice!

Be sure to put your feet in the right place; then, stand firm! Abraham Lincoln

"Rejoice" may be a new word for you. It means, "to be full of expressed joy." It is joy that cannot be contained.

Happiness is the goal for many folks. They simply want a happy life. Happy is a level of enjoyment and satisfaction that is far, far below joy.

Joy approaches the indescribable—"*Yippee-Skippee!*"—that is, an overwhelming feeling that can only be partially comprehended rationally. The wise know it exists, and it is acceptable to skip putting it all into words.

A song from my youth was "I Sing With Joy And Gladness." The songwriter points out the life-changing, life-giving **good news** of Jesus. Another fantastically satisfied customer. "Jesus is the real deal!"

Knows Up! This joy is immediately available and improves with age. It is such a fantastic problem to acquire, You cannot contain the *JOY* Jesus gives to His followers!

When God removes things from your life that are bad for you, don't go chasing after them.

Coffee Break!

Laughter is an instant vacation.

The early bird can have the worm;
I'll take my coffee!

> Are you at the stage of life where your train
> of thought leaves the station without you?

Sometimes I stay up so late that I have my morning
coffee before I go to bed.

> Some listen half, understand quarter,
> think zero, and react double!

No questions until
I've had my second cup of coffee!

> In memory of sleep—so suddenly
> taken from us by the alarm clock.

Laughter is a tranquilizer with no side effect.

Farewell

"Knows Up!"

A big thank you for hanging in there until the end. The "fun-o-meter" went off several times for me. I hope you enjoyed reading along as much as I learned that work can be fun.

The anticipation of attacking a project brings a big adrenaline rush. My mind goes a hundred miles an hour producing a plethora of ideas and possibilities. The novelty quickly wears off and the writing and rewriting takes over.

After reading and rereading, even Professor OB1 gets a little buggy-eyed. It dawned on me that I needed to stiff Professor Perfection. My belief is that the readers are smart enough to get the message in amongst the words, and are purposeful in their pursuit of wisdom.

Self-doubt is a part of everyone's mindset. My prayer is that some wisdom has resulted from your efforts in completing your reading and reflection. Everyone is working out his or her own answers on wisdom and the mystery of life. Blessings and *knows up!*

The sun eventually sets on a perfect day, your favorites end with mixed feelings, and the reality of tomorrow seems to come knocking a little early. So, as I head off into the proverbial sunset, I leave a few tidbits.

I hope you agree that wisdom takes the high road, pursuing the noble and best of everything available. Paul, the Apostle, jots down a list of wise and valuable traits when he writes:

> "Finally, brothers, whatever is true, whatever is honorable, whatever is just, whatever is pure, whatever is lovely, whatever is commendable, if there is any excellence, if there is anything worthy of praise, think about these things."   Philippians 4:8 (ESV)

We recognize that while we cannot block out all the noise and riff-raft demanding our attention, we can choose the ways that the wise pursue the excellent and best. Keep your eyes on the prize and finish strong.

Peter, another of the Apostles, describes the process and the result of developing and living wisdom. Our choices and their implementation really make a difference in our lives and in the lives of others. Peter shares:

> "For this very reason, make every effort to supplement your faith with virtue, and virtue with knowledge, and knowledge with self-control, and self-control with steadfastness, and steadfastness with godliness, and godliness with brotherly affection, and brotherly affection with love. For if these qualities are yours and are increasing, they

keep you from being ineffective or unfruitful
in the knowledge of our Lord Jesus Christ."

2 Peter 1:5-9 (ESV)

It is a real treasure and blessing the treasure trove of
wisdom that is available to those who nobly pursue the
best. Your paradigms and philosophy of life are lived out
in the reality of daily living. Your behaviors speak
volumes. Choose and act wisely.

You really do get one of two things in life: results or
excuses. All your behaviors and thoughts are your choices.
Keep taking the high road to wisdom.

It is commonly referred to as St. Francis of Assisi's
Prayer. While the author identity might be a little
uncertain, there is no question as to the wisdom for
individuals and all mankind.

> Lord, make me an instrument of Your peace;
> Where there is hatred, let me sow love;
> Where there is injury, pardon;
> Where there is error, the truth;
> Where there is doubt, the faith;
> Where there is despair, hope;
> Where there is darkness, light;
> And where there is sadness, joy.
> O Divine Master, Grant that I may not so
> much seek to be consoled, as to console;
> To be understood, as to understand;
> To be loved, as to love.
> For it is in giving that we receive;
> It is in pardoning that we are pardoned;
> And it is in dying that we are born to eternal
> life.

(Author unknown, but it is often called
The St. Francis of Assisi Prayer)

Let me close with a story I have shared all my life, all across the world. It contains the truth that we can make a difference.

> The ocean storm had deposited many starfish up on the beach. When the water receded, the starfish faced almost certain death. Starfish cannot live on the sandy beach. Walking down the beach immediately after the storm, a couple was picking up starfish and putting them back in the ocean. Walking up the beach, a man came by and asked the couple, "With so many starfish stranded on the beach, what difference does it make?" The wife held out a starfish and calmly answered, "It matters to this starfish," as she put another starfish into the ocean so they could continue living.

We are the starfish in this story. Wisdom is the couple putting the starfish back in the ocean. We individually, along with all mankind, benefit greatly from the benefits of wisdom. Wisdom is not a collection of noble, life-giving thoughts. We have a grocery store of the best foods available, but we must take and digest food so it becomes a living part of us.

So, too, with wisdom. Wisdom only benefits you and all mankind when it is ingested, digested, and lived out from day to day. Proceed.

Love, hugs, prayers, and blessings to all. Now, go pay it forward!

Why Books, Wood Crafts, and Quilts?

Proceeds from Tom and Donna's creative efforts go to help fund their travels to befriend, encourage and train Young Life leaders across Russia and the former Soviet Union.

This summer Tom and Donna went to Ukraine to help at a Young Life summer camp. They spent the month of October traveling to seven cities from St. Petersburg to Krasnodar, Russia.

Meeting with Young Life leaders in Ararat, Armenia, in the shadows of Mt. Ararat. Wonderful, caring, creative leaders befriending young people for Jesus Christ.

Compassion is difficult to give away: it keeps coming back.

In our 13 trips, the main blessing we receive is seeing the "joy of the Lord" in these first generation followers of Jesus. They live out the best of Jesus, and the best of Young Life. While we seek to encourage them, we also receive a tremendous blessing.

182

It has been a real education seeing what it means to follow Jesus in other countries and cultures. In the midst of their challenges, they continue to demonstrate an optimistic, loving outreach. They are great *"frienders."*

Being a Christian is not an extra-curricular activity on your resumé.

Donna continues to bring joy to newlyweds, new parents and leaders. Quilts are a reminder that friends deeply value who they are and what they are doing.

Please continue to pray that the Lord will provide for the needs of Young Life in the former Soviet Union, grant them favor in all ways, and bless their efforts as they continue to befriend and love young people.

"Do not feel totally, personally, irrevocably, responsible for everything. That's my job! Love, God"

Bibliography

Leman, Kevin. *The Way of the Wise: Simple Truths for Living Well.* Grand Rapids: Revell, 2013.

McDowell, Josh. *Evidence That Demands a Verdict.* Nashville: Thomas Nelson, 1992.

Mitchell, Robert. *Letters to a Young Life Leader.* Houston: Whitecaps Media, 2012.

Olson, Ken. *The Art of Hanging Loose in an Uptight World.* Fawcett World Library, 1974.

Ortberg, John. *Who is This Man?* Grand Rapids: Zondervan, 2012.

Stott, John. *Why I Am a Christian.* Downers Grove: InterVarsity Press, IVP Books, 2003.

White, John. *The Fight.* Downers Grove: InterVarsity Press, IVP Books, 1976.

www.brainyquote.com

www.ingramcontent.com/pod-product-compliance
Lightning Source LLC
Chambersburg PA
CBHW061432040426
42450CB00007B/1019

PRAISE FOR TOM SWANSON

Having just written a book on wisdom, I highly recommend *Blowing Your Knows In Public: From Smart to Wise.* As a former teacher, coach, and Young Life leader, Tom Swanson brings a wealth of insights to the process of moving towards wisdom. His easy to read, witty, light-hearted style will keep you turning pages. With some 300 one-liners, you will laugh and chuckle your way towards improving your "skill at living."

Dr. Kevin Leman, psychologist,
New York Times Bestselling author,
radio and television personality

I really enjoyed Tom's book. I am at a point in life where mentoring the next leaders of tomorrow is a big priority. This book gives great advice and insights toward that goal. Thanks, Tom!

Jeff Foxworthy,
Comedian, author, and TV host,
"Are You Smarter than a 5th Grader?"

Tom Swanson has practiced a lifetime habit of remembering those great one-liners that stick to the brain and inform the heart. His newest book offers further reason why such pithy wisdom is that which most often lingers and informs. As an old friend of mine used to say, "The only place you start at the top is digging a ditch." Tom didn't start at the top, but his modern proverbs offer not a ditch but a big pile of inspiration.

Dr. Lee Corder, Sr. Vice President
Young Life International North

What is your wisdom baseline? How do you take what you know and use it to define who you are? Tom Swanson's new book is more than a self-help book. It's a self-realization tutorial, backed by accumulated wisdom of hundreds of well-chronicled observations. "Aha" reading at its best.

Dennis Prikkel,
retired Fundraising Executive, Lutheran Church,
retired Grand Poobah and Bon Vivant

WARNING: Do not read Tom Swanson's charming little book, *Blowing Your Knows in Public,* unless you want a collection of one-liners to get stuck in your mind and change your heart forever!

Bob Stromberg,
Comedian

Tom Swanson was my teacher and coach back in the early '70's, and his one-liners have stuck in my head over the years. His life-long dedication to teaching us about life and to coaching us to be our best has come to delightful fruition in his book, *Blowing Your Knows in Public.* Take a happy walk with Tom from smart to wise, wear your laughing shoes, and see the journey of your life in a new light.

Thomas O'Hare, teacher,
University of Montreal

The premise of growing from smart to wise has a message of universal relevance. Written in his folksy,